impact

2A

SERIES EDITORS
JoAnn (Jodi) Crandall
Joan Kang Shin

AUTHOR
Katherine Stannett

Australia • Brazil • Mexico • Singapore • United Kingdom • United States

Thank you to the educators who provided invaluable feedback during the development of *Impact*:

EXPERT PANEL

Márcia Ferreira, Academic Coordinator, CCBEU, Franca, Brazil

Jianwei Song, Vice-general Manager, Ensure International Education, Harbin, China

María Eugenia Flores, Academic Director, and **Liana Rojas-Binda**, Head of Recruitment & Training, Centro Cultural Costarricense-Norteamericano, San José, Costa Rica

Liani Setiawati, M.Pd., SMPK 1 BPK PENABUR Bandung, Bandung, Indonesia

Micaela Fernandes, Head of Research and Development Committee and Assessment Committee, Pui Ching Middle School, Macau

Héctor Sánchez Lozano, Academic Director, and **Carolina Tripodi**, Head of the Juniors Program, Proulex, Guadalajara, Mexico

Rosario Giraldez, Academic Director, Alianza Cultural, Montevideo, Uruguay

REVIEWERS

BRAZIL

Renata Cardoso, Colégio do Sol, Guara, DF

Fábio Delano Vidal Carneiro, Colégio Sete de Setembro, Fortaleza

Cristiano Carvalho, Centro Educacional Leonardo da Vinci, Vitória

Silvia Corrêa, Associação Alumni, São Paulo

Carol Espinosa, Associação Cultural Brasil Estados Unidos, Salvador

Marcia Ferreira, Centro Cultural Brasil Estados Unidos, Franca

Clara Haddad, ELT Consultant, São Paulo

Elaine Carvalho Chaves Hodgson, Colégio Militar de Brasília, Brasília

Thays Farias Galvão Ladosky, Associação Brasil América, Recife

Itana Lins, Colégio Anchieta, Salvador

Samantha Mascarenhas, Associação Cultural Brasil Estados Unidos, Salvador

Ann Marie Moreira, Pan American School of Bahia, Bahia

Rodrigo Ramirez, CEETEPS- Fatec Zona Sul, São Paulo

Paulo Torres, Vitória Municipality, Vitória

Renata Zainotte, Go Up Idiomas, Rio de Janeiro

CHINA

Zhou Chao, MaxEn Education, Beijing

Zhu Haojun, Only International Education, Shanghai

Su Jing, Beijing Chengxun International English School, Beijing

Jianjun Shen, Phoenix City International School, Guangzhou

COSTA RICA

Luis Antonio Quesada-Umaña, Centro Cultural Costarricense Norteamericano, San José

INDONESIA

Luz S. Ismail, M.A., LIA Institute of Language and Vocational Training, Jakarta

Selestin Zainuddin, LIA Institute of Language and Vocational Training, Jakarta

Rosalia Dian Devitasari, SMP Kolese Kanisius, Jakarta

JAPAN

John Williams, Tezukayama Gakuen, Nara

MEXICO

Nefertiti González, Instituto Mexicano Madero, Puebla

Eugenia Islas, Instituto Tlalpan, Mexico City

Marta MM Seguí, Colegio Velmont A.C., Puebla

SOUTH KOREA

Min Yuol (Alvin) Cho, Global Leader English Education, Yong In

THAILAND

Panitnan Kalayanapong, Eduzone Co., Ltd., Bangkok

TURKEY

Damla Çaltuğ, İELEV, Istanbul

Basak Nalcakar Demiralp, Ankara Sinav College, Ankara

Humeyra Olcayli, İstanbul Bilim College, Istanbul

VIETNAM

Chantal Kruger, ILA Vietnam, Hô Chí Minh

Ai Nguyen Huynh, Vietnam USA Society, Hô Chí Minh

impact

2A

	1 Colour Matters	**2** Feeling Good?	**3** Your Virtual Self	**4** Underwater Mysteries
THEME	Colour and its effect on people	Body and mind	Technology's impact on our lives	Underwater exploration and discovery
VOCABULARY STRATEGIES	· Suffix *-al* · Use context clues	· Suffix *-ness* · Use a dictionary: Sample sentences	· Prefix *inter-* · Use a thesaurus	· Prefix *pre-* · Use context of unit
SPEAKING STRATEGY	Correcting information	Asking after friends and saying how you feel	Checking for understanding and responding	Making and responding to suggestions
GRAMMAR	**Comparatives and superlatives:** Comparing two or more things *Purple is a popular colour. Green is more popular than purple. Blue is the most popular colour in the world.* **The:** Identifying general and specific things *The sun is shining in the sky.*	**Adverbs:** Saying how and how often you do something *Many teenagers often like to sleep. They're always tired.* **Make + adjective:** Saying what affects mood and feelings *A lack of sleep makes you tired.*	**Modals:** Expressing obligation, advice and permission *You have to protect yourself with a strong username and password.* **Must, might** and **can't:** Expressing certainty *I checked the facts on three different websites, so they must be true.*	**Used to and would:** Talking about habits in the past *I never used to be interested in the sea, and I didn't use to read much at all!* **Past simple:** Describing past actions *When did the village sink? It sank thousands of years ago.*
READING	*Purple Power*	*The Teenage Brain*	*Calm Down*	*Yonaguni Jima*
READING STRATEGY	Identify sequence of events	Summarise	Connect text to personal experience	Identify author's purpose
VIDEO	*Seeing Colours?*	*The Forgotten Organ*	*The Distance Between Two Points*	*Loch Ness Monster: Mystery Solved?*
WRITING	Genre: **Descriptive paragraph** Focus: Topic sentence	Genre: **Classification essay** Focus: Introducing categories	Genre: **Fact and opinion essay** Focus: Facts and opinions	Genre: **Contrast essay** Focus: Contrasting points of view
MISSION	**Look for Opportunities** National Geographic Photographer: **Annie Griffiths**	**Take Care of Yourself** National Geographic Explorer: **Pardis Sabeti**, Computational Geneticist	**Connect with People** National Geographic Explorer: **Amber Case**, Cyborg Anthropologist	**Be Curious** National Geographic Explorer: **Katy Croff Bell**, Oceanographer
PRONUNCIATION	The schwa /ə/ sound	Pronunciation of *-s* endings	*Have to*	Verb *use* vs. *used to* + verb
EXPRESS YOURSELF	Creative Expression: **Song** *One Truth* Making connections: How colours affect your body and mind		Creative Expression: **Blog** *The* Nautilus *Expedition to the Cayman Islands* Making connections: Technology's impact and ocean exploration	

Unit 1

ANNIE GRIFFITHS Photographer

Annie Griffiths was one of the first women photographers for *National Geographic*. She fell in love with photography when she studied it in college. She has worked in more than 100 countries taking colourful pictures of people and places.

Unit 2

PARDIS SABETI Computational Geneticist

Pardis Sabeti was born in Tehran, Iran. She is the lead singer and bass player in a rock band. She's also a computational geneticist. Pardis works to understand and control dangerous diseases like Ebola. She wants to keep the world healthy, and she knows that, in order to do that, people need to work together. They need to share information, understand other people and have fun!

Unit 3

AMBER CASE Cyborg Anthropologist

How do humans and technology interact? Amber Case is on a mission to find out. As a cyborg anthropologist, she studies the relationship between people and technology. Amber looks at how the use of gadgets and computers affects our lives in both positive and negative ways. How does technology affect your life?

Unit 4

KATY CROFF BELL Oceanographer

Katy Croff Bell is an underwater detective! As an oceanographer, Katy uses deep-sea technology to explore the ocean. She spends much of her time aboard the E/V *Nautilus* as it travels the world's seas. She's excited to share her work with the rest of us using *telepresence* technology. With this technology, we can use computers to explore with Katy as she makes discoveries on the ocean floor.

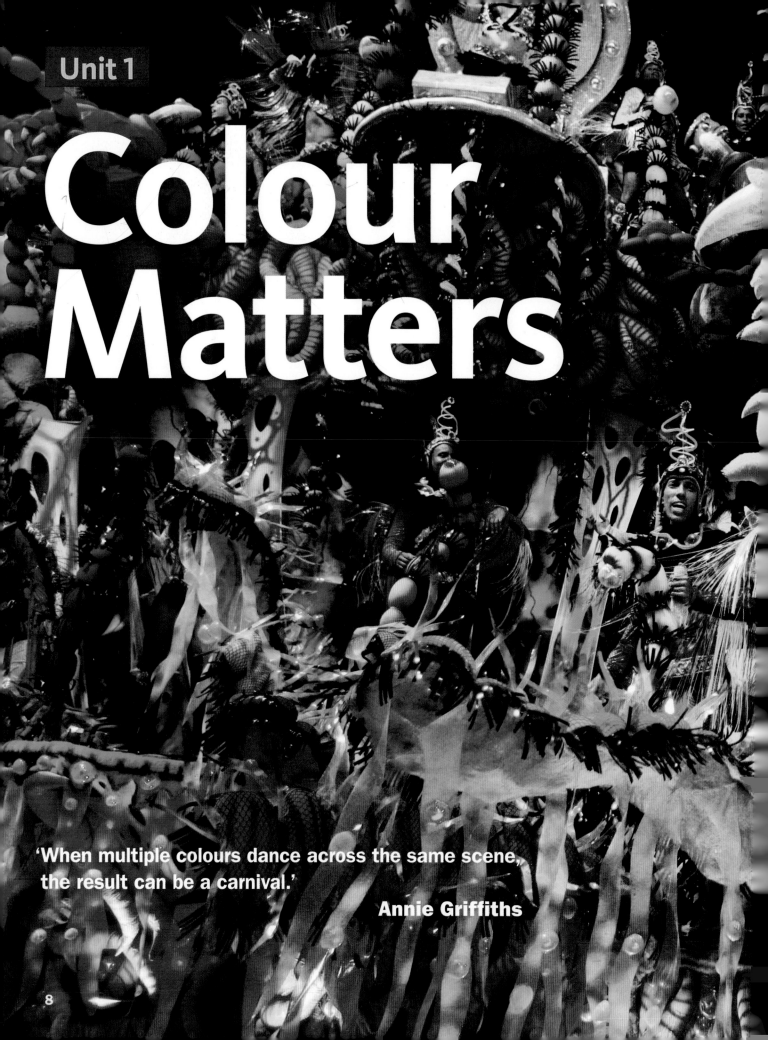

Colour Matters

'When multiple colours dance across the same scene, the result can be a carnival.'

Annie Griffiths

People celebrating Carnival
in Rio de Janeiro, Brazil

TO START

1. Name all of the different colours that you can see in the photo. Which is your favourite?

2. Would you like to be at the place in the photo? Why or why not?

3. Imagine this photo in black and white. What would you think of it? What would be lost?

9

1 Your brain can see seven million colours. How many of them can you name? What do different colours make you think of? Discuss. Then listen and read. ⌒ 002

RED is a symbol of **good luck** in many cultures. It is the traditional colour for **wedding** dresses in China and India. But many cultures associate red with **danger**. This is why we see it on **emergency** vehicles and warning signs. Eight per cent of the population is red-green **colour-blind**: they can't clearly see the difference between red and green.

GREEN is a colour that makes people feel at peace because it's the most common colour in nature. The green in leaves and grass comes from something called *chlorophyll*. This word comes from the Greek *khloros* (green) and *phyllon* (leaf).

Green also symbolises **safety**. Because of this, it's used in traffic lights to signal when it's safe to go.

BLUE is the most popular colour in the world. More than half the world's flags have blue in them. Blue is also the most common colour used by businesses. Many businesses use the colour blue to **represent** them in logos and advertisements. This is because blue helps us feel like we can **trust** them.

ORANGE gets its name from the fruit. The word originally described the taste of the fruit's peel, but by the 16th century, *orange* was also the name of this **bright** colour.

YELLOW is the colour of taxis and school buses in many parts of the world because it's the most **visible** colour on the road. Like red, yellow is also used to **warn** people of dangerous situations. Because it attracts attention, yellow is used for highlighter pens. The bright colour activates different parts of the brain that help the reader remember the highlighted text.

INDIGO is a dark colour between blue and purple. Indigo clothing was a sign of luxury in the past because indigo **dye** came from a rare plant. It was very expensive, and few people could wear clothes made with this dye. Now we use indigo dye to make blue jeans.

VIOLET is a **light** purple colour. It is one of the oldest colours in the world. There are violet cave paintings in France that are 25,000 years old! However, in some countries, for example Thailand and Brazil, violet is the colour of **death**.

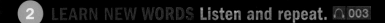

2 LEARN NEW WORDS **Listen and repeat.** 🎧 003

3 **Work in pairs.** Which colours make you feel happy? Sad? Angry? Excited?

4 **Read and write the words from the list.** Make
any necessary changes.

bright	danger	light	represent
safety	visible	war	wedding

Photographer Annie Griffiths has
travelled all around the world. In many
of the places she's visited, Annie has seen
_____ . However, Annie
chooses to focus on the beauty of the places and
the people she meets. This photo is one of her favourites. It shows her son resting next to
her friend. She took it after a _____ celebration in Jordan. For Annie,
the photograph expresses her son's feeling of _____ and happiness.

Annie loves to use _____ colours in her photos. She says, 'It's
difficult to photograph a very dark thing, for example the black fur of a panther, or a very
_____ thing, for example a snowy field. But one spot of colour in a
picture can make it look amazing.'

5 **LEARN NEW WORDS Listen to these words and match them
to the definitions.** Then listen and repeat. 🎧 004 005

Photographer
Annie Griffiths

common	flag	luxury	signal

1. _____ give a sign or a warning
2. _____ happening often
3. _____ a special thing
4. _____ the symbol of a country

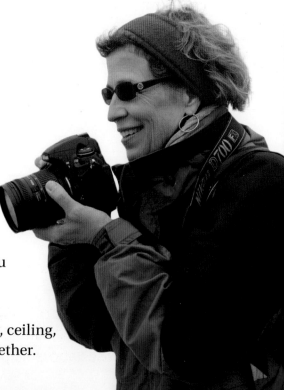

6 **YOU DECIDE Choose an activity.**

1. **Work independently.** Choose a favourite photograph
   and show it to the class. Describe the photo and talk
   about its colours. Explain why you like it so much.

2. **Work in pairs.** Discuss the saying: *A picture is worth a
   thousand words.* What do you think this means? Do you
   agree with it? Why or why not?

3. **Work in groups.** Your teacher asks you to paint your
   classroom. Which colours will you choose for the walls, ceiling,
   desks and chairs? Why? Create a design suggestion together.

Correcting information

The sky is blue.	Actually, <u>it isn't blue</u>.
	As a matter of fact, <u>the light from the sun is lots of colours</u>.
	In fact, <u>we see blue because blue light rays are shorter than light rays of other colours</u>.
	After all, <u>the sky changes from blue to red when the sun sets in the evening</u>.

1 **Listen.** How do the speakers correct information? Write the words and phrases you hear. 🎧007

2 **Read and complete the dialogue.**

Jaime: White is the most popular colour for wedding dresses.

Ana: _____ , it isn't a popular colour everywhere.

Jaime: Really?

Ana: Yes. _____ , white is the colour of death in China, Korea and other Asian countries.

Jaime: Wow, I didn't know that.

Ana: _____ , red is the colour of weddings and celebrations in India and China.

Jaime: Interesting! I think red is a great colour for wedding dresses.

_____ , it is a symbol of love in many cultures!

3 **Work in pairs.** Place all of the cards on the desk with the photos facing up. Both students take cards with matching photos. One partner reads information, and the other corrects it.

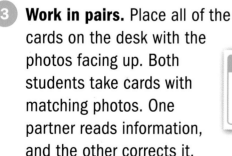

Correct by saying:

A polar bear's fur isn't white. It's clear. It reflects the light and this makes it look white.

Go to page 153.

Polar bears have got white fur.

As a matter of fact, their fur isn't white. It's clear, but it reflects the light. This makes it look white.

4 **Work in groups.** When is it important to correct information? What do you need to consider when correcting what someone else says? How do the words and phrases above help you to communicate better?

GRAMMAR ⌂008

Comparatives and superlatives: Comparing two or more things

Adjective	Comparative	Superlative
Purple is a **popular** colour.	Green is **more popular than** purple.	Blue is **the most popular** colour in the world.
Green peppers are **tasty**.	Red peppers are **tastier than** green peppers.	Yellow peppers are **the tastiest** peppers.
Red grapes are **good**.	Red grapes are **better than** green grapes.	Red grapes are **the best**.

1 **Read.** Choose the correct word or phrase to complete the paragraph.

hungrier	larger	most delicious	sweeter	worse

When you see your favourite food on a red plate, you probably feel hungry. But you feel

_____ when it's on a white plate. Why? Research shows that colours

can really affect our feelings about food. For example, when you add red dye to water, it tastes

_____ than normal water, as if you've added sugar. The food that you

think is the _____ will probably taste _____

to you if you change its colour to blue. This is because blue is a very unnatural colour for food.

Colour can also affect how much we eat. In one experiment, people were asked

to serve themselves some pasta with white sauce. The people with red plates

took a small portion, while the people with white plates took a much

_____ portion. Can you guess why this happens?

2 **Read.** Complete the sentences with the correct comparative or superlative forms. Then listen and check your answers. ⌂009

1. Dark green vegetables are _____ (high/low) in vitamin C than light green vegetables.

2. Yellow bananas are _____ (salty/sweet) green bananas, but green bananas are _____ (good/bad) for you.

3. Blue is _____ (common/unusual) colour for food.

4. _____ (healthy/popular) diet includes foods of many different colours.

3 **Work in pairs.** Make a list of your five favourite foods. Then share your list. Make comparisons about those foods.

> Apples are better for you than biscuits, but biscuits are sweeter!

4 LEARN NEW WORDS Listen and read to find out about colours and moods. Then listen and repeat. 🎧 010 011

We make strong **connections** between colours and feelings.

GREEN **RELAXED**

RED **NERVOUS**

BLUE **DEPRESSED**

5 Work in pairs. Discuss how you feel when you see these things.

I feel relaxed when I see green trees.

I feel nervous when I see red lights on a car.

Me, too! But I feel more relaxed when I look at blue artwork.

6 Work in groups. Compare your answers to Activity 5 with another pair. Then choose two other colours and say how they make you feel.

PURPLE POWER
THE HISTORY OF ONE OF THE MOST POPULAR COLOURS

Purple is one of the most popular colours today. There are purple clothes, purple handbags, purple bicycles, purple furniture, even purple computers! But in the past, purple was a very expensive and unusual colour.

Let's take a look at the rich and sometimes dangerous history of the colour purple.

THE VERY BEGINNING

Some scientists believe that the first organisms to appear on Earth over 500 million years ago probably looked purple, not green. Plants today are green because they use green chlorophyll to produce energy. But these early organisms probably used something called *retinal,* which is a dark purple colour.

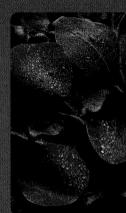

1 BEFORE YOU READ **Discuss in pairs.** Look at the photos and the timeline. What do you think the reading is about?

2 LEARN NEW WORDS **Find these words in the text.** Use the other words in the sentences to guess each word's meaning. Then listen and repeat. 🎧 012

| company | notice | ordinary | royalty |

3 WHILE YOU READ **Think about the order of the events.** 🎧 013

4 AFTER YOU READ **Discuss in pairs.**

1. Why do scientists think that the earliest organisms were purple?

2. Why was the colour purple so expensive during the Roman Empire?

3. Who usually wore purple in England in the 16th century?

4. How did William Perkin discover a way to make purple dye? What advantage did his discovery have?

3,000 YEARS AGO

During the time of the Roman Empire, it was very difficult to make purple dye. The dye came from sea snails. But 10,000 dead sea snails got you just one gram of purple dye ... as well as a very bad smell! This special purple dye was called *Tyrian purple,* and it was the preferred colour of emperors.

500 YEARS AGO

In 16ᵗʰ-century England, purple was only for royalty. Queen Elizabeth I's clothes were purple, but ordinary people were not allowed to wear the colour.

150 YEARS AGO

In 1856, William Perkin, an 18-year-old science student, noticed something strange while conducting an experiment. The chemicals he used to clean his equipment combined with the chemicals he used in his experiment and produced a bright purple colour. This discovery led Perkin to start a company using this chemical combination to make purple dye. The dye was much cheaper than the sea-snail dye. Thanks to Perkin, now anyone can wear purple clothes.

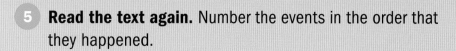

5 **Read the text again.** Number the events in the order that they happened.

_____ Only Queen Elizabeth I wears purple clothes.

_____ Sea snails are used to make purple clothes for emperors.

_____ Many of the Earth's plants appear to be purple, not green.

_____ Anyone can wear purple clothes.

_____ William Perkin discovers how to make purple dye.

6 **Discuss in groups.**

1. What colour clothes do you like wearing? Why?

2. In Roman and Elizabethan times, purple was a sign of luxury. What colour means luxury to you? Does the colour purple have any special meaning in your culture?

3. Why do some people like to have luxury items, such as clothing? Are luxury items important to you? Why or why not?

1 **BEFORE YOU WATCH Discuss in pairs.** How do we use colour in our life? Think about ways that colour warns or informs us about things.

2 **Work in pairs.** You're going to watch a video called *Seeing Colours?* Look at the photo. How many different colours can you see? Do you think that all animals see colours the same as you do?

3 **WHILE YOU WATCH Write the letter for each colour in order, based on the range of visible light.** Watch scene 1.1.

a. dark blue   b. green   c. infrared   d. light blue   e. orange   f. red   g. ultraviolet   h. violet   i. yellow

4 **AFTER YOU WATCH Work in pairs to answer the questions.**

1. Why don't insects and animals see colours like most humans do?

2. What can bees see in flowers that is invisible to humans?

3. How can a snake see a mouse in the dark?

4. What colour is infrared light to a snake?

5. What percentage of men are colour-blind? What percentage of women are colour-blind?

5 **Work in pairs.** Choose one of these gadgets and find out how it uses infrared light. Share your answer with the class.

- TV remote control
- supermarket check-out scanner
- night-vision goggles
- car keys

A mouse visible in a *thermogram*, an image that shows an object's temperature

6 **YOU DECIDE** Choose an activity.

1. **Work independently.** Find pictures of things in nature that match each colour in the range of visible light. Arrange the pictures in order on a sheet of paper and glue them. Then label each item and its colour.

2. **Work in pairs.** Go online to find out why you see a rainbow when it rains on a sunny day. Give a presentation to explain the science.

3. **Work in groups.** How important is colour in your life? Can you imagine a life without colour? What problems might there be? List at least three.

The: Identifying general and specific things

There's a coat in my wardrobe. **The** coat is red.

The sun is shining in **the** sky.

People often feel depressed when they see **the** colour black.

---

1 **Read.** Circle the correct word.

The / A Colours of Success

Imagine you're at a shopping centre. You want to go to *the / a* café and get *the / a* drink and *the / a* snack. There are two different cafés in the shopping centre. How do you choose *the / a* café you want to visit? You probably look at the prices and the menus. But *the / a* colours that *the / a* cafés use are also very important.

Do you want to feel calm and relaxed? Then you will probably choose The Coffee Place. *The / A* green colour makes you think of nature and peace.

Do you want to go somewhere exciting and lively? Then you will probably choose The Coffee Machine. Many companies use *the / a* colour red because it seems bright and fun, and it attracts young people.

Think about your favourite brands. Which colours do they use? What do those colours mean to you?

2 **Work in pairs.** Take turns naming familiar brand-name products. Can your partner name the colours for the brand? Why do you think the companies chose the colours for each product?

3 **Work in pairs.** Take turns. Use a coin to move (heads = 1 space; tails = 2 spaces). Complete each sentence with *the* or *a / an*.

Go to page 155.

WRITING

A topic sentence introduces the main idea of a paragraph. The topic sentence is usually the first sentence of the paragraph. It explains:

- why you are writing
- what you want to say

Look at these examples of topic sentences:

In this article, I'm going to discuss the history of the colour orange.
When taking a photograph, it's important to think about light and colour.

1 **Read the announcement and the response.** Underline the topic sentence.

COMPETITION

Write and tell us about your favourite colour.

What colour do you want to see at home and around town this season? Tell us what the colour means to you.

I would like to tell you about my favourite colour and explain why I think it's perfect for this season. My favourite colour is orange. I think it's a warm and bright colour, and it makes me feel happy and safe. When I see this colour, I think of the autumn. Although it gets cooler and the days are much shorter, I love the autumn. When I go outside, I enjoy walking through the dark orange leaves and listening to the sound they make under my feet. I also think of the smell of fire when I see this colour. It's great to be at home and sit by the warm fire with my family. Orange is also the colour of my favourite food – carrot soup. It's so delicious! This warm and beautiful colour should be everywhere this season – outside, in our homes and even on our plates!

2 **Work in pairs.** Make a list of the things that the writer connects with his/her favourite colour. Do you think his/her ideas are effective? Why or why not?

3 **Write.** Write a paragraph about your favourite colour and what you associate with this colour. Use a strong topic sentence.

Look for Opportunities

'Look around and ask yourself, 'Who needs pictures? Who needs help?' With photography, the opportunities are endless ...'

Annie Griffiths
National Geographic Photographer

1. **Watch scene 1.2.**

2. Discuss how photographers can use their skills to help other people.

3. Think about issues or social problems in your area. How could you use photographs to teach others about these issues?

Make an Impact

1 Plan and create an art presentation.

· Research the use of colour in Aboriginal art.

· Draw an object from your own culture using Aboriginal art techniques.

· Present your drawing to the class. Explain why you chose the colours you used.

2 Plan and give a presentation about colour and taste.

· Choose five foods. Use food colouring to change each food's colour.

· Ask friends and family to taste and react to the foods.

· Present the results to the class.

3 Blog about colours in your community.

· Find colourful people, places and things in your community. Take photos of them.

· Write a blog about your photos. Explain why you took each photo and how the colours make you feel.

· Publish your blog and respond to your classmates' comments.

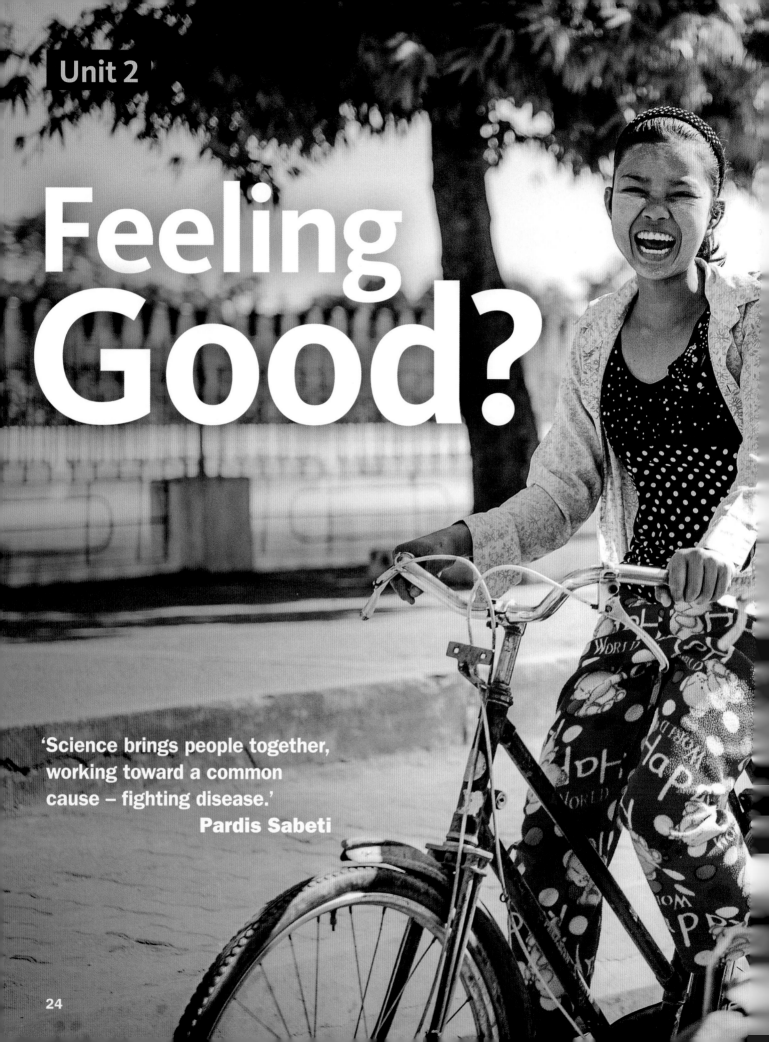

Unit 2

Feeling Good?

'Science brings people together, working toward a common cause – fighting disease.'
Pardis Sabeti

Girls on bikes in Mandalay, Myanmar

TO START

1. Look at the girls in the photo. How do you think they feel? Why do you think they feel this way?

2. How has science helped to improve people's health over the last 100 years? Give examples.

3. Work in small groups to think of three ways in which science affects your daily life. Share your ideas with the class.

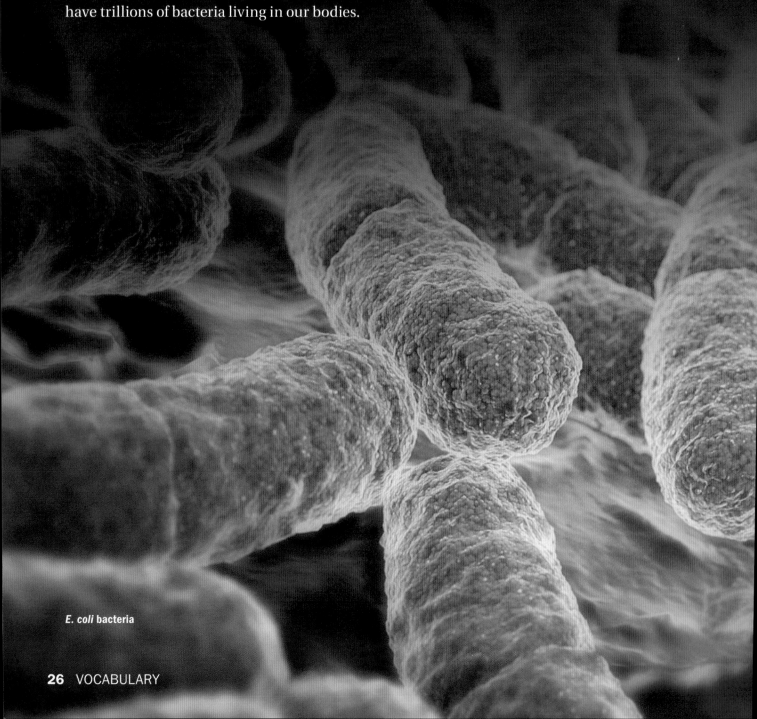

Discuss. Then listen and read. ∩ 015

How are you feeling today? Have you got a **sore** throat? Are you coughing? Sneezing? These are all very common **symptoms** that signal your body is fighting a **disease**. Your **immune system** works to protect you from diseases, but when it is weakened, you feel ill. The illness that you feel could be caused by one of two things: **bacteria** or **viruses**.

Bacteria are organisms with just one **cell**. They can survive outside the body, but we also have trillions of bacteria living in our bodies.

In fact, there are more bacteria than human cells in our bodies. But don't worry: 99 per cent of these bacteria are good for us. They allow us to feel positive emotions, **protect** us from disease and help us **digest** food. Your mouth alone contains more bacteria than there are people on Earth! Unfortunately, there are also bad bacteria that cause illnesses. We can **treat** these bacterial **infections** with **antibiotics**.

E. coli bacteria

Viruses are smaller than bacteria. They cannot exist without a host – an animal or plant to live in. That person next to you who's sneezing? She's the host of a virus, so watch out! With each sneeze, she sends you over 100,000 virus cells, travelling at a speed of over 160 kph. (100 mph.)! Once those cells **invade** your body, you become the host. The virus then changes in order to make more viruses in your body. If you get a virus, you can't treat it with antibiotics. You simply need to wait until your body gets rid of it. Of course, you can protect yourself from viruses such as the flu by getting **vaccinations**, or even just by washing your hands. Over 80 per cent of viruses are spread by touching an infected person or thing, so make sure you take care of yourself and stay healthy!

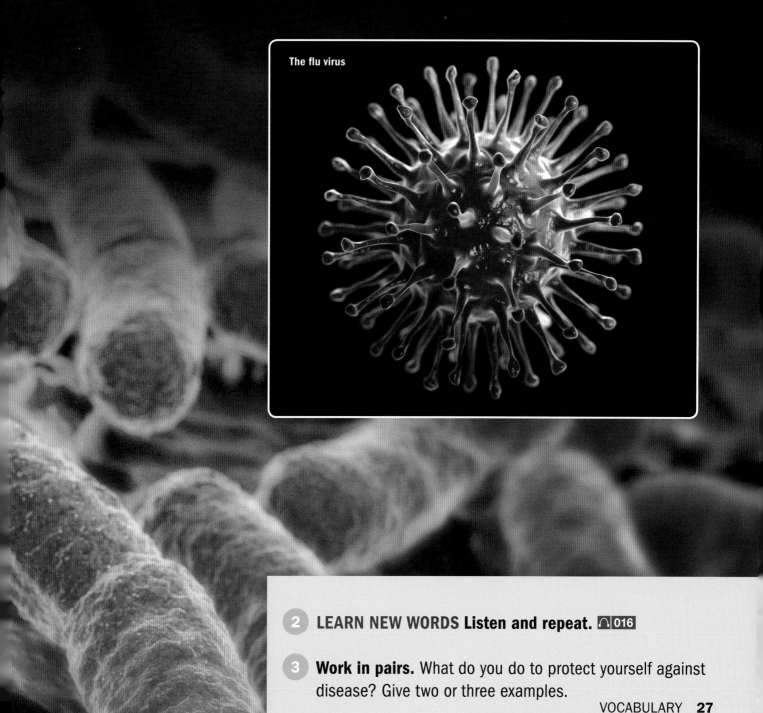

The flu virus

2 **LEARN NEW WORDS Listen and repeat.** 🎧 016

3 **Work in pairs.** What do you do to protect yourself against disease? Give two or three examples.

4 **Read and circle the correct word.**

Pardis Sabeti is a doctor and a researcher. In her recent research on the *antibiotic / virus* that causes Lassa Fever, she wanted to find out why some people get the *disease / cell* and others don't. Pardis didn't just do research in her lab. She travelled to hospitals in Africa to learn more about diseases. There, she helped train medical workers to *treat / digest* people. She hopes that one day her research will help scientists to make a *symptom / vaccination* available that can *protect / invade* people against Lassa Fever.

5 **LEARN NEW WORDS Listen to these words and match them to the definitions.** Then listen and repeat. 🎧 017 018

emotion	illness	positive	survive

_____ 1. state of being ill

_____ 2. confident and happy

_____ 3. continue to live

_____ 4. feeling

6 **YOU DECIDE Choose an activity. Work in pairs.**

1. Make a list of three health problems in your country. Then write the causes of these problems.

2. Pardis is hardworking and creative. Do you have either of these traits? If so, what do you use them for?

3. If you could find the cure for one disease, which disease would it be and why? Discuss. Then share your responses with the class.

Scientist Pardis Sabeti is also in a rock band, Thousand Days.

Asking after friends	Saying how you feel
Are you OK?	Yes, I'm fine. / Not really. I feel <u>awful</u>.
Are you feeling better?	Yes, I'm starting to. / No, I feel worse. I need <u>to go home</u>.
Is anything wrong?	No, everything's OK. / Actually, I'm feeling a bit ill.

1 **Listen.** How does Myriam ask after her friend? Write the phrases you hear. 🎧 020

2 **Read and complete the dialogue.**

Yuto: Hey, Aiko. _____

Aiko: Actually, _____

Yuto: That's a shame! Do you want to go to the nurse?

Aiko: That might be a good idea. _____

Yuto: Come on, I'll walk with you.

            (A little while later …)

Aiko: Hi, Yuto. Thanks for your help earlier.

Yuto: No problem. _____

Aiko: Yes, _____ I think

            that by tomorrow, I'll feel fine.

3 **Work in pairs.** Play Noughts and Crosses.
Choose X or O. Then choose a square, and use
the words on that square to ask after your friend.
Mark your letter (X or O) for a correct sentence.
Then your friend chooses a square and responds
to your question. Try to get three in a row.

> Is anything wrong?
> Actually, I'm feeling a bit tired.

tired	need	better
OK	go home	worse
wrong	feel	ill

4 **Work in groups.** Why is it important to talk to friends about how you feel? Do you
ever feel like you don't want to tell a friend how you feel physically and emotionally?
How could you politely express this?

GRAMMAR 🎧021

Adverbs: Saying how and how often you do something

Many teenagers **often** like to sleep. They're **always** tired.
Many people **rarely** get enough sleep. They can get ill more **easily**.
If you sleep **regularly**, you're **usually** able to pay more attention at school.

1 **Read and circle the correct word.**

If you're like a lot of teens, you like sleeping. And that's a good thing! But many people sleep *always / badly* , and this has harmful effects on the body and mind. While you sleep, your body *well / regularly* produces cells that work to fight infections. If you don't sleep *enough / easily* , fewer cells are produced and your immune system doesn't work as *effectively / always* . As a result, you can become ill more *rarely / easily* .

Lack of sleep also affects your mind. You're more likely to feel angry or depressed, so you react *negatively / usually* to almost everything. A lack of sleep makes it difficult to pay attention *rarely / carefully* to what's happening in school. Making good decisions, solving problems and remembering things *always / poorly* seems much harder when you don't get a good night's sleep. Lack of sleep also makes you react to things more *sometimes / slowly* . In fact, tired drivers may be responsible for around 20 per cent of all traffic accidents. Sleeping at least seven hours a night is important for your health, your marks and even your safety!

2 **Work in pairs.** You learnt that sleep is important. Talk about the benefits of sleeping well. Use words from the box in your discussion.

| always | calmly | clearly | effectively | often | regularly | usually |

A good night's sleep helps me think clearly.

3 **LEARN NEW WORDS** **Read and listen to information about the connection between sleep and intelligence.** Then listen and repeat. 🎧 022 023

Researchers that study sleep and the **brain** have a **theory**: getting enough **rest** is strongly connected with intelligence. Just as humans prefer to sleep in **comfortable** beds, highly intelligent animals like these chimpanzees **select** the strongest trees for a good night's sleep.

4 **Work in pairs.** Talk about your own sleep habits. Do you sleep well? What affects your sleep? Why? Use the words in the box to help you.

badly	comfortable	enough	nervous
rest	select	stress	well

5 **Work in groups.** Design a bedroom that would result in really good sleep. Draw your design. Explain why the room is good for getting enough sleep. Use adverbs to talk about how the room helps people sleep. Present your information to the class.

1 BEFORE YOU READ **Discuss in pairs.** Based on the title and the image, what do you think this reading is about?

2 **LEARN NEW WORDS Find these words in the reading.** What do you think they mean? Use a dictionary to check. Pay attention to how each word is used in a sentence in the dictionary. Then listen and repeat. 🎧 024

adolescent	experience	process	structure

3 WHILE YOU READ **Summarise each paragraph.** 🎧 025

THE
Teenage Brain

Shaping your future

1 Being a teenager can be challenging, but it can also be exciting. You're becoming more independent and making decisions for yourself. You are also learning to take risks and solve problems better than you could before. And changes are happening throughout your body, even in your brain.

2 You can't see the changes in your brain, but they're affecting how you develop into an adult. At this time in your life, there is a process going on inside your brain that makes it work faster and more efficiently. Imagine that the structure of your brain is like a big road map. There are lots of roads leading to different destinations. When you were a child, as you learnt new things, your brain created more and more roads leading to different destinations. By the time you become an adolescent, the most important places on the map have many different roads leading to them. Now your brain's job is to make that map more efficient. It removes the roads that you don't need and works to make the other roads faster.

3 As a result, your experiences as a teenager actually affect the way that your brain develops. If you spend hours playing video games, what skills do you use? You learn to see something with your eyes and respond to it with your hands. As you develop those skills, your brain is making sure that the roads leading to them are especially fast and efficient. So, your video-game playing could be preparing you for a career such as a fighter pilot, or even a surgeon.

4 This is a great time for you to practise new skills and discover what you're good at and what you love doing. Go out and try different activities, and stick with them if you think they're useful. Remember that with everything you do, you're shaping your brain for the future.

4 **AFTER YOU READ** Work in pairs to answer the questions.

1. What does the writer compare the structure of the brain to?
2. What happened to your brain as you learnt new things as a child?
3. How does the brain become more efficient when you are an adolescent?
4. How can your experiences as a teenager affect the development of your brain?
5. What is the writer's advice for teenagers?

5 **Match these summaries to the correct paragraph.** Write the number on the line.

_____ What you do as an adolescent affects your brain's development.

_____ Your brain forms many connections when you are a child, and then it makes them more efficient when you are a teenager.

_____ It is important to try to have lots of new experiences when you are a teenager.

_____ Teenagers experience a lot of changes.

6 **Discuss in groups.**

1. How do some of the activities you enjoy doing now provide you with important skills for the future? Give examples.

2. Knowing that what you do shapes your brain, what activities shouldn't you do? Why shouldn't you do them? Give one or two examples.

3. Name three interesting careers. Then imagine what activities a teenager could do now to shape their brains for each career.

VIDEO ▷

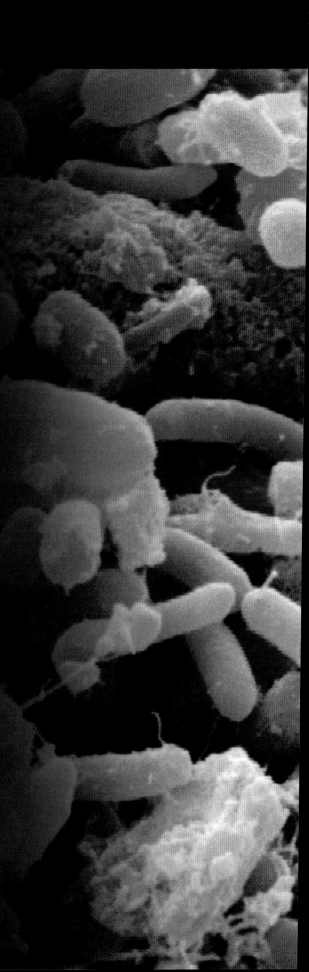

1 BEFORE YOU WATCH **Discuss in pairs.** How can each of the following affect your emotions?

diet	health	other people
school	sleep	surroundings

2 **Work in pairs.** The title of this video is *The Forgotten Organ.* An *organ* is a part of the body with a special task, such as the heart. What do you think the 'forgotten organ' is? Discuss your ideas.

3 WHILE YOU WATCH **Answer the questions.** According to the video, what is the 'forgotten organ'? Was your answer from Activity 2 correct? Watch scene 2.1.

4 AFTER YOU WATCH **Work in pairs to answer the questions.**

1. What are microbes?

2. What part of your body is almost equal in weight to all the microbes in your body?

3. How many bacteria are in your gut?

4. How do the microbes in your gut send signals to your brain?

5. When Elaine Hsiao observed communication between two mice, what did she notice about the mouse with no microbes?

6. What happened when she put microbes back into the mouse?

5 **Work in groups.** Some bacteria and viruses are harmful. Discuss examples of harmful microbes. Describe a time when harmful microbes made you ill. How did you treat the situation?

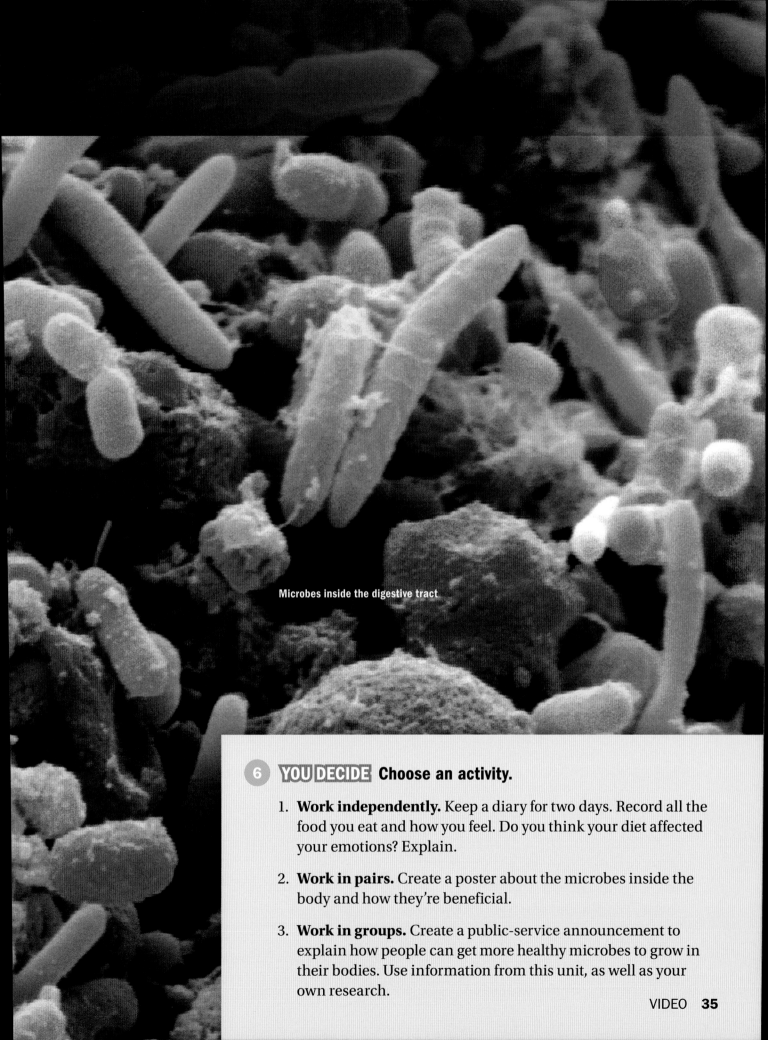

Microbes inside the digestive tract

6 **YOU DECIDE** **Choose an activity.**

1. **Work independently.** Keep a diary for two days. Record all the food you eat and how you feel. Do you think your diet affected your emotions? Explain.

2. **Work in pairs.** Create a poster about the microbes inside the body and how they're beneficial.

3. **Work in groups.** Create a public-service announcement to explain how people can get more healthy microbes to grow in their bodies. Use information from this unit, as well as your own research.

Make + adjective: Saying what affects mood and feelings

A lack of sleep **makes** you tired.

Does exercise **make** you feel good?

Some viruses **make** us very ill.

Can this medicine **make** you better?

1 **Read.** Complete the sentences to say how these things make people feel.

🐦 📌 📘 📷

Today we want to know all about you. What makes you feel the way you do?

I love running, and I am on the school's track team. Exercise ___makes me tired___, 😮

but it also _____ ! 🙂 **Jamie (13)**

Fast food _____ . 😖 I really love how it tastes, but I always
have a stomach ache after I eat it! **Paolo (13)**

Seeing people with terrible viruses _____ . 🙁 I hope that
scientists can find a way to treat them. **Julia (14)**

Tests _____ . 😬 I can't sleep the night before an important
one. It's awful! **Brad (11)**

Watching my favourite football team _____ . 😄 Their games are
always fun to watch. **Will (12)**

2 **Work independently.** Use *make* to say how each of the following affects you.

1. A strong immune system _____ *makes me feel healthy.* _____

2. A virus can _____

3. Good bacteria can _____

4. A good night's sleep _____

3 **Work in pairs.** Take turns
throwing the cube. Say what
makes you feel the emotion.

A good video game makes me excited.

Really? Video games make me feel
bored. Action films make me excited.

Go to page 157.

WRITING

When we write a classification essay, we divide the topic into different categories. Then we present each category and support it with examples. The following phrases are useful when classifying:

additionally   **another type/way**   **to begin with**   **the final type/way**

1 **Read the model.** Work in pairs to identify the different categories in the essay. Underline words that signal the categories.

When people hear the word *stress*, they usually think of something negative. However, stress can have several benefits for the body and mind. To begin with, there is the type of stress people feel when there is something important to do. For example, some students are stressed before a big test. The stress might make them feel nervous, but it also makes them feel focused. This type of stress can help people work efficiently to meet their goals.

Another way stress benefits us is by keeping us healthy. Scientists who study stress learnt that a little stress strengthens the immune system. When your body learns to respond to some stress, it's able to protect you from infection better.

The final way that stress benefits us is by helping us react to danger. If you see a car coming around the corner too fast, you might experience stress. This stress sends a message to warn your brain of danger, allowing your body to respond quickly. Without the stress, you may not be able to jump out of the car's way soon enough.

Of course, too much stress is harmful to our bodies and minds. But the right amount of stress makes us more efficient, healthier and safer.

2 **Work in pairs.** What are the three benefits of stress mentioned in the essay?

3 **Write.** Write a classification essay about the negative effects of stress. Give examples.

NATIONAL GEOGRAPHIC

Take Care of Yourself

'Taking care of others can only happen if you first take care of yourself.'

Pardis Sabeti
National Geographic Explorer, Computational Geneticist

1. **Watch scene 2.2.**

2. Pardis says that you first have to take care of yourself before you can help others. Do you agree with her? Why or why not? Do you take care of yourself? What could you do to improve?

3. How do you balance work and fun in your life? What are your daily responsibilities? What do you do for fun? Do you have enough time for both? Explain.

Make an Impact

YOU DECIDE Choose a project.

1 **Create a brochure about healthy living.**

· Find out about the importance of sleep, vaccinations, exercise and healthy food.

· Organise your findings in a brochure. Include photos and drawings.

· Present your brochure to the class.

2 **Plan and conduct sleep research.**

· Write five questions to find out how well your classmates sleep.

· Survey at least ten classmates. Summarise the results.

· Present the information to the class.

3 **Plan and hold a microbial quiz show.**

· Prepare cards with different facts about viruses and bacteria.

· Organise two teams in your class.

· Hold the quiz show. Read each fact aloud. Classmates say if you're describing a virus or bacteria.

Express Yourself

1 Read and listen to the song *One Truth* by Pardis Sabeti's band, *Thousand Days*. 🎧 027

ONE TRUTH

I'm sitting in here in this room
Watching everything move
I do not know how this city was built
We are forsaken to the sound
Oh that life that goes
But we were born to radiate

We are gathered on the ground
Waiting for a sign to arrive
Looking for the answers in the
    starry sky
But we were home all along
    and we are the light
We think, we speak, we walk, we
    breathe the air

Yeah
A lifetime that we write
We laugh
We cry
We pray
We are love
We dream
We scream
We strive
Our hunger will never die
I'm here in this fight, always

A lifetime for one for one truth
That I'm alive, And so are you
We are here, We are the proof
Yeah

A lifetime for one
For one truth

2 Discuss in groups.

1. Pardis recorded this song with other
   scientists while fighting the Ebola
   virus. They saw many people, including
   friends, die of the virus. This made
   them very sad. To help, they recorded
   this song. What is the 'one truth' that
   they are singing about?

2. Do you like the song? Why or why not?

3 Connect ideas. In Unit 1, you learnt
about colours. In Unit 2, you learnt about
health. What is the connection between
these two units? How can colours affect
your body and your mind?

4 YOU DECIDE Choose an activity.

1. Choose a topic:
   • how colours make you feel
   • body and mind

2. Choose a way to express yourself:
   • a song
   • a poem
   • a piece of graphic art

3. Present your work.

Unit 3

Your Virtual Self

'Really good technology helps us all be more human and connect with each other as we never could before.'

Amber Case

This girl is wearing a high-tech armband that can find her friends nearby, send text messages and even act as a video-game controller.

TO START

1. Look at the photo. Have you ever used anything similar to this type of technology? Explain.

2. What technology do you use in your daily life? Think about your home, your schoolwork and your free-time activities.

3. Imagine you don't have a mobile phone. How would you contact your friends? Explain.

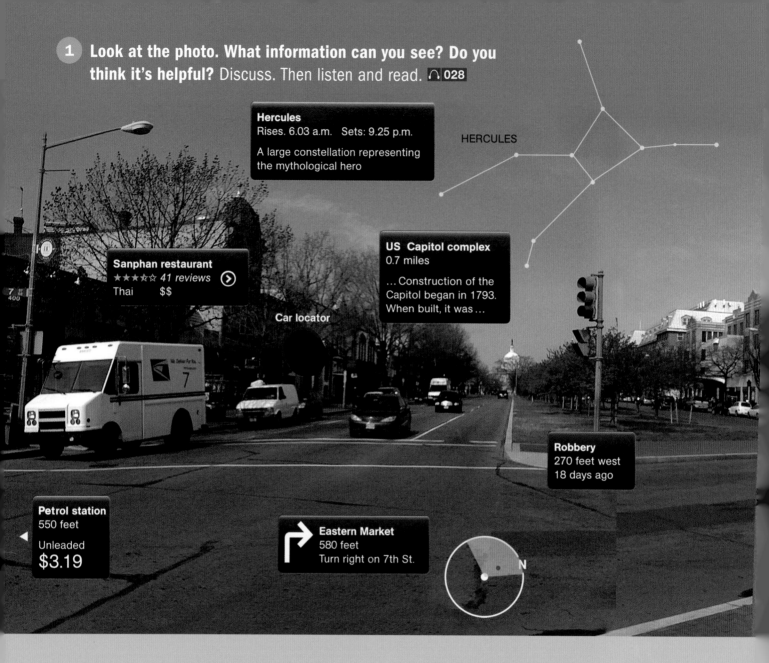

1 **Look at the photo. What information can you see? Do you think it's helpful?** Discuss. Then listen and read. 🎧 028

Hercules
Rises. 6.03 a.m.   Sets: 9.25 p.m.
A large constellation representing the mythological hero

HERCULES

Sanphan restaurant
★★★☆☆ 41 reviews ⊙
Thai $$

Car locator

US Capitol complex
0.7 miles
... Construction of the Capitol began in 1793. When built, it was ...

Robbery
270 feet west
18 days ago

Petrol station
550 feet
Unleaded
$3.19

↱ **Eastern Market**
580 feet
Turn right on 7th St.

Anthropologists traditionally study human behaviour and culture. They look at the way humans live and work together. Amber Case is an anthropologist, but she studies a different type of anthropology. Amber is a cyborg anthropologist. Do you know what a cyborg is? Part human, part **machine**, a cyborg is usually associated with science fiction films or comic books.

Amber believes that in today's **digital** world, we're all cyborgs. We rely on **technology** all the time. Our mobile phones and tablet computers are like extra body parts that we carry around with us. 'Our mobile phones have become like children,' explains Amber. 'If they cry, we pick them up. We plug them into the wall and feed them. When they're lost, we panic.'

In the past, we humans developed **tools** that extended our physical **abilities**. We used them to **improve** the environment, farm the land, move around faster or protect ourselves. In the 21ˢᵗ century, our smart tools – our gadgets – extend our mental abilities. With

In the 21st century...

44 VOCABULARY

622–624 North Carolina Ave. SE
900 feet

List price: **$2,995,000**
Bed: **7**   Bath: **8**
On market: **420 days**

flickr: Eastern Market Fire
510 feet

Taken: 30-04-2007
09.35 a.m.

Peregrine Espresso
195 feet

Free Wi-Fi

Bus stop
70 feet

Nearest for

32 34 36

A11 C40

CIRC

Twitter users in the area

perfect day to head to @EasternMarketDC
anyone want to meet up? #spring #dc #market
Posted by @ARpro 10 minutes ago

Subway stop
140 feet

Nearest for
⊕ Orange Line
● Blue Line

modern technology, we can **communicate** faster and find any **information** we want in an **instant**. **Social media** allows us to connect with people around the world. So friendships can form based on our shared interests, not just our **location**.

Although there are a lot of positive things about technology, Amber thinks there is also a negative side to our new cyborg selves. She worries that our **constant access** to other people interferes with our ability to just be alone. Wherever we are, there's someone we know who's online and ready to interact with us. 'We aren't taking time to slow down and figure out who we really are,' says Amber.

Despite these concerns, Amber doesn't think that machines are taking over. 'We're sharing with each other – human to human – in a very real way.'

2 LEARN NEW WORDS **Listen and repeat.** ∩ 029

3 **Work in pairs.** Do you agree that you're a cyborg? Why or why not?

4 Read and write the words from the list.

access	communicate	constant	digital
information	location	social media	technology

According to Amber Case, in today's world of _____ , people have two selves. There's the real self, and then there is a second self – the _____ self. This is the person that you become when you go online. There are some risks to having a virtual identity. Through your virtual self, you create huge amounts of _____ about yourself that anyone can _____ . Another problem is that you're never really alone. People still _____ with your virtual self when you're not there. Even when you're sleeping, your friends are using their smartphones to connect with you on _____ . This _____ online interaction means it's very difficult to disconnect!

5 LEARN NEW WORDS Listen to these words and match them to the definitions. Then listen and repeat. 🎧 030 031

extend	interfere	rely on	take over

_____ 1. take control of

_____ 2. make something larger

_____ 3. feel that you can't be without

_____ 4. get in the way of something

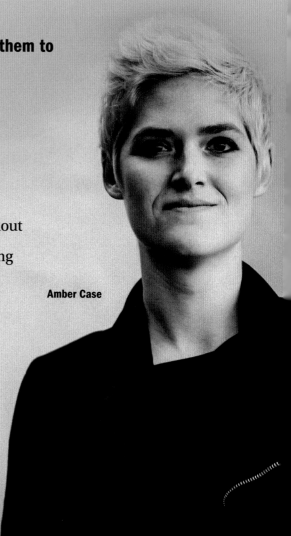

Amber Case

6 YOU DECIDE Choose an activity.

1. **Work independently.** Do you think modern technology has made us better at communicating? Write a paragraph to explain your opinion.

2. **Work in pairs.** Discuss a piece of technology that has really changed your life. How has it made your life easier?

3. **Work in groups.** Discuss. How often did you communicate with friends and family online in the last week? Imagine you don't have a mobile phone or a computer. How would you communicate with your friends and family?

Checking for understanding	Responding
Do you mean that <u>cars will drive themselves in the future</u>?	That's right. <u>There are already self-driving cars on the road</u>!
So, you're saying that <u>mobile phones will replace</u> <u>computers</u>?	Not quite, but <u>we'll be able to do even more on our phones</u>.
Do you actually believe that <u>we won't need to write by hand</u>?	That's exactly what I mean. <u>No one will need pencil and paper in the future</u>.

1 **Listen.** How do the speakers check that they understand each other? Write the phrases you hear. 🎧033

2 **Read and complete the dialogue.**

Carla: Twenty years from now, I doubt that anyone will have a mobile phone.

Santana: Seriously? Do _____ that we won't talk on the phone in the future?

Carla: No, _____ . I just think that we'll have technology in our brains. So then we won't need to carry anything with us.

Santana: _____ that we'll all have tiny machines in our heads?

Carla: _____

Santana: No way! I don't agree. I think we'll have more wearable technology.

Carla: Wearable technology? _____ mean things like special glasses or watches?

Santana: Yes. That's _____ . These gadgets are already out there. But in the future, they'll be much cheaper so that anybody can buy them.

Carla: Maybe you're right. And I like that better than the idea of a machine in my head!

3 **Work in pairs.** Spin the wheel to make a prediction about the topic you land on. Your partner will check for understanding.

People won't drive in the future.

Do you mean that cars won't need drivers?

That's right.

4 **Discuss in groups.** Why is it important to check that you understand something? What might happen if you get the wrong idea about what someone is saying?

Go to page 157.

GRAMMAR 🎧 034

Modals: Expressing obligation, advice and permission

You **should** be careful about your safety online. You **shouldn't** give away personal information.

Students **don't have to** ask to use the computer, but they **must** ask if they can go online.

You **have to** protect yourself with a strong username and password.

Can anyone use the computer at the library? You **can/may** only use the Internet if you have a library card. Children under 14 **can't/may not** use the Internet at all.

1 **Read.** Circle the correct answer.

The Internet is great, and it gives you the ability to do a lot of things. You *can / should* learn about some really interesting topics and find people who have the same interests as you. But at the same time, you *must / shouldn't* always think about what you say and do online. You *don't have to / should* remember that real people with real feelings are reading your words. You *should / can't* behave the same way online as you behave in real life. Everyone says mean things sometimes, but when you write something online, it will always be there for everyone to see. You *may / have to* say things you don't believe, but you *can / can't* ignore other people's feelings. When you talk to people in real life, they can see your face and your body language. Online, they just read your words, so you *can't / have to* be very careful about the words you choose.

2 **Work in pairs.** Write advice using *can, may, should, must* and *have to*.

1. Someone is mean to you online.

   _____

2. A stranger sends you a message on social media.

   _____

3. You want to start your own blog.

   _____

4. Someone uses a photo of you without asking you first.

   _____

3 **Work in groups.** Take turns discussing problems at school or online. Give advice using *can, may, should, must* or *have to*.

> I forgot my password for the school website.

> You should send an e-mail to the computer teacher.

4 **LEARN NEW WORDS Listen to learn about online safety.** Then listen and repeat. 🎧 035 036

Your personal information should always be **private.** Don't share it with strangers!

You must choose your **username** and your **password** carefully.

Identity **theft** happens when someone **hacks** into your account and uses your personal information.

A good username and password can protect your information and provide **security**.

5 **Work in pairs.** Imagine that you want to start a new social media website. How can you make sure that it's safe? Make a list of five guidelines for users to follow. Use the words in the box, as well as *can, may, should, must* and *have to.*

hack	information	password	private	theft	username

1. _____

2. _____

3. _____

4. _____

5. _____

6 **Discuss in groups.** People hack into businesses, banks, government websites and personal e-mail accounts. What information do they want to find? What can they do with this information? What should you do if your own account gets hacked?

1 BEFORE YOU READ **Discuss in pairs.** Based on the title, the photo and the graphics, what do you think the reading is about?

2 LEARN NEW WORDS **Find these words in the reading.** What do you think they mean? Use a thesaurus to find synonyms for each word. Then listen and repeat. 🎧037

demand	edge
focus	interrupt

3 WHILE YOU READ **Think about your own home and the technology you use there.** 🎧038

4 AFTER YOU READ **Look at the sentences.** Tick T for *true* or F for *false*.

1. Amber Case invented the idea of calm technology. (T) (F)

2. Calm technology demands our attention at all times. (T) (F)

3. A smoke alarm is an example of calm technology. (T) (F)

4. Cooking your food on the hob is an example of calm technology. (T) (F)

5. Amber believes that houses in the future will use calm technology. (T) (F)

5 **Work in pairs.** List three examples from your life where technology has demanded your attention. Then list three examples of calm technology in your school or home. Share your responses with the class.

Calm Down

Should we be excited about calm technology?

Often it seems like technology is everywhere. Computers and smartphones are at the centre of almost everything we do. They're constantly demanding our attention. We text our friends during the day, sleep with our devices by our beds and check our messages as soon as we wake up.

According to Amber Case, in the future, technology will no longer be interrupting us all of the time. Instead, we will use calm technology – a concept first developed by scientist Mark Weiser in the 1970s. In his vision, calm technology works quietly but constantly, at the edge of our attention. We know it is there, but we don't focus on it. According to Mark, the best technology should be invisible and let you live your life.

We already use many different types of calm technology in our everyday lives. Do you have a smoke alarm in your house? That smoke alarm is always there, checking the air for smoke and quietly keeping you safe. It only reminds you it's there when you've burnt your toast! Or there may be lights in your home or school that are sensitive to movement. When somebody passes in front of their sensor, the lights turn on. You don't think about this type of technology until you see the light go on. Even a microwave oven is an example of calm technology. You're not standing at the hob heating your food: the microwave is doing it for you. You don't think about its work until you hear the beeping noise signalling that your food is ready.

In the future, Amber imagines that our houses will use calm technology to open the curtains for us in the morning, to turn down the heat when we leave, or even to choose the best music for our mood. The minute we walk through the door, our house will respond by turning on the lights and music, setting the radiators to a comfortable temperature and perhaps even starting to prepare our dinner!

6 **Discuss in groups.**

1. Amber believes that eventually, with calm technology, electronic devices will do all the boring, repetitive tasks in our lives. How will this benefit us? What negative impact might this have on us?

2. Calm technology will allow different machines in our lives to share information about us, our routines and our personal habits. Do you think that sharing this information is a security risk? Why or why not?

3. Design a house that uses calm technology. Think of all the ways it can use calm technology to make our lives easier without demanding our attention.

VIDE▶

1 BEFORE YOU WATCH Discuss in pairs.

1. When you're communicating with your friends, does speed matter? Do you expect your friends to respond instantly? Why or why not?

2. When might you want to slow communication down? Why?

2 Work in pairs. You are going to watch a video called *The Distance Between Two Points*. Before you watch, do the following:

1. Draw two points on a sheet of paper. Label them *A* and *B*.

2. Now draw the shortest route from point *A* to point *B*.

3. How could you make this route even shorter?

3 WHILE YOU WATCH Check your responses
How does Amber say the distance between two points is made shorter? Does your response from Activity 2 match what she says? Watch scene 3.1.

Singers joining in a virtual choir

4 AFTER YOU WATCH **Read the sentences.** Circle the correct answer.

1. Amber's dad said that a straight line *was / wasn't* always the shortest distance between two points.

2. Amber thinks technology *reduces / creates* the distance between two people.

3. Amber studies how technology *affects culture / must be used all the time.*

4. With *calm technology / social media*, others can interact with our virtual selves when we're not there.

5. Amber created an interface that tells her phone when *she's at home / her family members are online.*

6. Amber believes that people *sometimes need distance from / need constant access to* one another.

5 **Work in pairs.** What technology might you use in each of the places below? When might it be a problem to use technology at each place?

gym	home	library
museum	school	

6 YOU DECIDE **Choose an activity.**

1. **Work independently.** Imagine you can send a letter back in time to your great-great grandparents. Write a description of a smartphone.

2. **Work in pairs.** Amber's phone has an invisible interface so that it knows when she's at home. How could your phone help you based on your location? What kinds of things could it do? Give at least three ideas.

3. **Work in groups.** Think about how communication has changed over the past 100 years. Create a timeline showing at least five ways that communication has changed. Then add two or three predictions for how communication will change in the future.

GRAMMAR 🔊 039

***Must*, *might* and *can't*: Expressing certainty**

I checked these facts on three different websites, so they **must** be true.

This website **must** mention security somewhere.

This **might** be her social media page. I'm not sure.

He **can't** be the author of this article: he doesn't know anything about the topic!

1 **Read.** The information below came from the Internet. Some sentences are true and some are false. Use *must*, *might* and *can't* to write what you believe.

1. Giant tortoises can live for one year without food or water. *That must be true! My own pet turtle can live without food for a while. / That can't be true! All animals need to eat and drink.*

2. There were computers during World War II. _____

3. You only use ten per cent of your brain. _____

4. On average, youngsters spend over 150 hours a week using technology. _____

5. There are robots that can play football. _____

6. More people die every year from vending machine accidents than from shark attacks. _____

2 **Work in groups.** Write two true sentences and one false sentence on a piece of paper. Read your sentences to the group. Can they guess the false sentence?

> Number 2 must be false. Your house can't be 100 years old – it's too modern!

1. My mum knows how to fly a helicopter.
2. My house is 100 years old.
3. I have 15 cousins.

Answers to Activity 1: 1. true; 2. true; 3. false (100%); 4. false (53 hours); 5. true; 6. true

WRITING

In an opinion essay, we want to tell others what we believe about a topic. We use facts to support our argument. We must make it clear when we're stating a fact and when we're expressing an opinion.

Facts include:
· a date or time of an event
· a statistic
· a description of an event

Opinions include what the author:
· believes is possible
· thinks about something
· says is good, bad, important, etc.

1 **Read the model.** Work in pairs. Circle the sentences stating facts. Underline the sentences expressing opinions.

An early personal computer

Can we live without computers?

For most people my age, it's hard to imagine life without a computer. It seems like almost everybody has got one! In fact, there are 640 million personal computers in households around the world. Most people use them every day for work and play. Actually, the first personal computer was invented in 1975. Before then, people survived without computers and the Internet, so it must be possible!

I believe that there would be some advantages to life without a computer. We would probably do more exercise because we wouldn't be sitting in front of our screens all day. Maybe we would get better at remembering things because we couldn't always check facts online. I think we would also interact more with each other because computers wouldn't demand so much of our attention.

However, I think that it would also be very difficult for young people today to live without computers. We use them to communicate with our friends and family all around the world. We also use computers to research information about many different subjects. Computer technology has helped improve our lives in many different areas. For example, mechanics use computers to check our cars, doctors use computers to analyse health tests, and architects use computers to design modern, safe buildings.

In conclusion, although I think that we may have had healthier lifestyles in our computer-free past, I believe that, in today's society, we can't live without computers.

2 **Work in pairs.** Do you agree with the writer's opinion? Think of one more argument against and one more argument in favour of life without computers. Use facts to support your arguments.

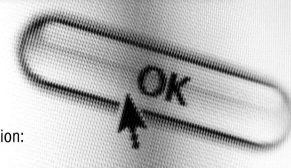

3 **Write.** Write an opinion essay to answer the question: Can we live without smartphones?

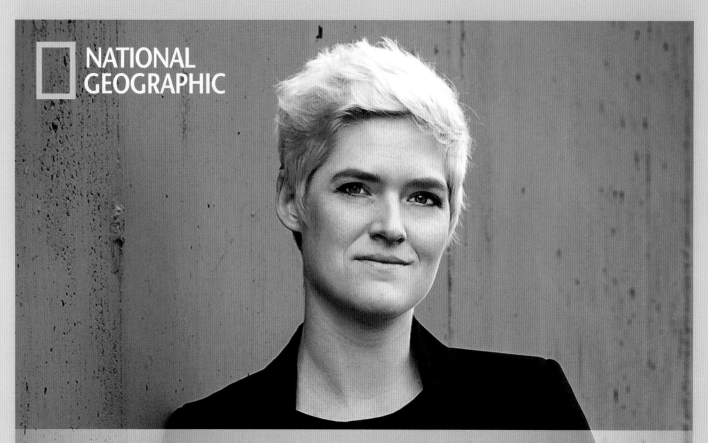

Connect with People

'Today's technology extends our mental self. It's changing the way we experience the world.'

Amber Case
National Geographic Explorer, Cyborg Anthropologist

1. **Watch scene 3.2.**

2. What are your favourite ways to connect with people now? Is it the same for everybody in your life? Explain.

3. How will technology change our communication in the future? Will it help or harm communication? Explain.

Make an Impact

YOU DECIDE Choose a project.

1 **Plan and conduct a survey.**

· Write questions to find out about your classmates' online activity.

· Conduct the survey and summarise the results.

· Present the results and make recommendations.

2 **Advertise an app or website.**

· Choose an app or a website that you use regularly.

· Write a list of its best and worst features.

· Create an advert for the app or website. Present it to the class.

3 **Plan and hold a technology fair.**

· In a group, bring in five or six different technological gadgets.

· Write a short description of each piece.
Display your descriptions with the gadgets.

· Hold a technology fair. Discuss
how each item is used with
your classmates.

Underwater Mysteries

'What's really exciting is having the
opportunity to explore anywhere in
the world, and share discoveries with
everyone in the world.'

Katy Croff Bell

Exploring a shipwreck near Key Largo, Florida, USA

TO START

1. Look at the photo and then read the caption. Does it surprise you? Why or why not? Would you like to explore something like this? Explain.

2. Why do people explore underwater? Think of as many different reasons as possible.

3. Imagine you can explore anywhere in the world. Where will you go? Why?

1 How can technology make underwater exploration easier? Discuss. Then listen and read. 🎧 040

Exploring underwater used to be very difficult. Every **expedition** would take careful preparation, and underwater explorers had no way to communicate with people on land. In fact, we landed on the moon before we started to explore our biggest underwater mountain range, the Mid-Oceanic Ridge. But thanks to technology, all of that is changing. Now, we can explore the deep sea without ever leaving home!

Katy Croff Bell is a leader on E/V *Nautilus* – a ship that explores the oceans. One week the **destination** might be the Gulf of Mexico, in an

attempt to find a shipwreck. The next week, *Nautilus* will be on a **journey** to investigate underwater volcanoes near Grenada. Scientists on the ship send robotic **vehicles** deep into the sea to **look for** shipwrecks, to study the plants and animals, and to look at the geology, or rocks, in an area. The vehicles transmit images and information back to the scientists on the ship. It's a great way to explore deep and dangerous places. And robots aren't the only cool technology on *Nautilus*.

Let's say you want to find out where *Nautilus* is at the moment. Well, you can go

E/V *Nautilus* uses robotic vehicles like this one to explore deep waters.

online to see. The *Nautilus* **website** has a 24-hour webcam so that people all around the world can find out what's happening on the ship at any time of day or night. Telepresence technology allows you to be a **virtual** explorer on *Nautilus*. You can also **follow** the updates on the *Nautilus* **blog** and send **messages** to scientists on the ship. Some people even get the **opportunity** to help out with the research! Scientists can communicate with **experts** on

the other side of the world and make sure that they have **accurate** information about their discoveries. For example, when researchers on *Nautilus* discovered an aircraft on the ocean floor near Sicily, World War II pilots helped them identify it. 'The telepresence system allows people from schoolchildren to research scientists to be a part of our expeditions,' says Katy. 'It's really exciting!'

2 **LEARN NEW WORDS** Listen and repeat. 🎧041

3 **Work in pairs.** Imagine you're communicating with the scientists on E/V *Nautilus*. What questions do you want to ask? What do you think the ship might discover during your virtual visit?

4 Read and write the words from the list. Make any necessary changes.

attempt	blog	destination	expert	journey
message	online	opportunity	virtual	website

In 2013, *Nautilus* was on a _____ through the Caribbean Sea. Its _____ was the Kick' em Jenny volcano, near the island of Grenada. The scientists were making an _____ to learn more about the volcano's last big eruption. But when they started to dive around the volcano, they discovered that chemicals from the volcano created a perfect environment for a lot of different organisms. It was a wonderful _____ for the scientists to study many underwater animals. _____ from all over the world read the *Nautilus* _____ and saw the video footage _____ . Then they sent _____ to *Nautilus*, asking for samples of all the different organisms. 'It was probably the most exciting dive of the season!' says Katy.

5 LEARN NEW WORDS Listen to these words and match them to the definitions. Then listen and repeat. 🎧 042 043

find out	make sure	preparation	transmit

Katy Croff Bell on E/V *Nautilus*

_____ 1. the act of getting ready

_____ 2. send a signal

_____ 3. learn something

_____ 4. check or confirm something

6 YOU DECIDE Choose an activity.

1. **Work independently.** What do you think a day in the life of a scientist on E/V *Nautilus* is like? What kinds of things do they do? Write a paragraph about a crew member's typical day.

2. **Work in pairs.** Deep-sea exploration is dangerous, difficult and expensive. With this in mind, make a list of five reasons why we should explore the deep sea.

3. **Work in groups.** Imagine you're a scientist on *Nautilus*. You have made an exciting discovery on the sea floor. What did you find? How did you find out more about it? How did you tell others? Share with the class.

SPEAKING STRATEGY 🎧 044

Making suggestions	Responding to suggestions
How about <u>going scuba diving</u>?	Yes, good idea! / I love that idea, but <u>it isn't a good time of year for that</u>.
It would be great to <u>follow *Nautilus* online for our next project</u>.	Sure. That's a really great suggestion. / Unfortunately, <u>my Internet connection isn't working at the moment</u>.
We could <u>research underwater volcanoes for the science fair</u>.	OK. Let's do that. / Yes, but <u>we did volcanoes for last year's presentation</u>.

1 **Listen.** How do the speakers make and respond to suggestions? Write the phrases you hear. 🎧 045

2 **Read and complete the dialogue.**

Ameira: Do we have any plans for tonight yet?

Nora: Not yet. _____ have a picnic on the beach.

Ameira: _____ , the weather forecast says it's going to rain tonight. It'll be too wet for a picnic. Any other ideas?

Nora: _____ go to the cinema. There's a great documentary about underwater exploration that I'd really like to see.

Ameira: _____ I don't really like documentaries.

Nora: OK, well _____ just staying at home and checking out the *Nautilus* live feed? The ship's in the Atlantic Ocean, and the crew is looking for shipwrecks near Portugal.

Ameira: Sure! That's a _____

3 **Work in pairs.** Throw the cube and make a suggestion for where to go on a holiday. Your partner will respond to your suggestion. Then swap roles.

> How about exploring an underwater shipwreck?

> I love that idea, but wouldn't that cost a lot of money?

4 **Work in groups.** Imagine that visitors from another country are coming to your school, and your class must show them around town. Make and respond to at least four suggestions about what to do with them.

Go to page 159.

GRAMMAR 🔊 046

Used to and ***would***: Talking about habits in the past

Did you use to read about the sea as a child?

No, I **never used to be** interested in the sea, and I **didn't use to read** much at all!

That changed when my dad, who **used to be** a diver, took me diving for the first time, and I saw an old shipwreck.

After that, I **used to / would read** anything about the sea I could get my hands on!

1. **Read.** Complete the sentences with *used to* or *would* and the verb in brackets.

In the past, when scientists wanted to do research in the seas, they _____ (go) out on a ship to collect their information.

Typically, the expeditions _____ (be) several weeks long.

After the expedition, scientists _____ (bring) their data home with them. They _____ (work) on that information for several months, and finally, they _____ (write) about their results in a scientific paper. Most people never read this information because it _____ (be) available only in scientific magazines or newspapers.

A 19th-century diving suit

2. **Work in pairs.** Use the information to rewrite sentences about sea exploration in the early 19th century. Use *used to* and *would*.

1. Scientists travelled underwater in submarines or diving bells.
   Scientists would travel underwater in submarines or diving bells.

2. Ships used wind power to travel.

   _____

3. Divers pulled on a lifeline to communicate with people above the water.

   _____

4. Divers were able to breathe with air pumped from the surface.

   _____

3. **Work in pairs.** Talk about your habits in the past.

did you use to	I didn't use to	I never used to	I would always/never	I used to

4 **LEARN NEW WORDS Listen to learn about the SS *Republic* and her final journey.** Then listen and repeat. 🎧 **047** **048**

SS *Republic*'s Final Journey

New York ●

SS *Republic* **set off** from New York on 18th October 1865.

SS *Republic* sank off the coast of Georgia. Years later, in 2003, marine archaeologists **succeeded** in finding more than 51,000 silver and gold coins from the sunken ship.

Savannah ●

New Orleans ●

Her destination was New Orleans – a **distance** of 3,148 km. (1,956 mi.). Unfortunately, she never **reached** it.

5 **Read and write the words from the list.** Use *used to* or *would* when possible. Make any other necessary changes.

be	distance	reach	set off	succeed	travel

In the 19th century, people _____ by ship more often because there were no aeroplanes. One ship, SS *Republic*, _____ from New York in 1865. Its destination was New Orleans. New Orleans was a great _____ from New York, and travelling by boat was never completely safe. Journeys such as this _____ difficult and sometimes dangerous because of the weather conditions. Most of the time, the ships _____ in arriving at their destination. However, this was not the case for SS *Republic*, which never _____ New Orleans. The ship sank near the coast of Savannah and wasn't found until 2003.

6 **Work in groups.** Talk about how life used to be for the people travelling on SS *Republic*. Discuss the topics below. Use *used to* and *would*.

- what they did in their free time
- why they carried gold coins
- what they ate
- how they travelled

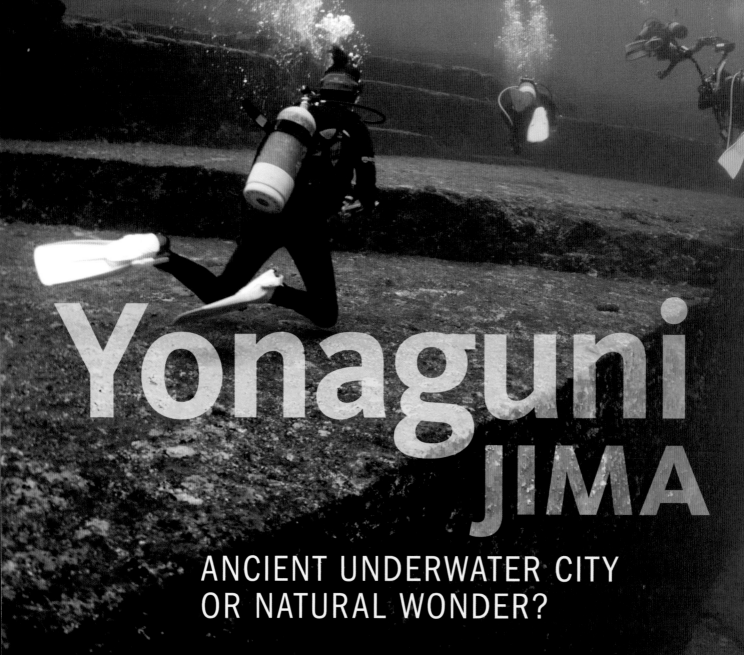

1 **BEFORE YOU READ Discuss in pairs.** Based on the title and the photo, what do you think the reading is about?

2 **LEARN NEW WORDS Find these words in the reading.** What do you think they mean? Think about the context of this unit and how the words connect to it. Then listen and repeat. 🎧 049

angle	carving	examine	identify	remains

3 **WHILE YOU READ Think about the author's purpose in writing this text.** 🎧 050

Yonaguni
JIMA

ANCIENT UNDERWATER CITY OR NATURAL WONDER?

Some believe it's an ancient city that sank thousands of years ago. Others think it is a natural structure – the result of many earthquakes in the area. Either way, the huge rock formations and stone structures off the coast of Yonaguni Island are an amazing sight.

The small Japanese island of Yonaguni is 1,029 km. (640 mi.) south of the coast of mainland Japan, between the East China Sea and the Pacific Ocean. From November to July, many divers visit Yonaguni to see the hammerhead sharks. In 1986, a local diver, Kihachiro Aratake, was looking for sharks about 18 m. (60 ft.) underwater when he discovered an enormous rock shaped like a rectangle. It was about the size of two football fields. There were huge steps on the rock, perfect right angles and long, straight passages. Was this really just a rock? Or was it something more?

Masaaki Kimura, a marine geologist, travelled to the island to examine the discovery. At first, he thought the formations were natural. But then he noticed shapes and carvings on the rock. Masaaki now believes that these rock formations are the remains of an important city more than 5,000 years old. He thinks that it sank in a huge tsunami about 2,000 years ago. Masaaki has identified the ruins of a castle, several temples and a large stadium in the rock formations.

Some scientists disagree with Kimura. Robert Schoch, also a geologist, thinks that earthquakes caused these rock formations and the 'carvings' are just natural scratches on the rock. 'I do not believe it is a human-made structure,' says Robert. 'It is absolutely incredible, and well worth seeing, but it is a natural structure.'

Perhaps we will never know the truth about Yonaguni. But one thing is for sure: it's an amazing place to explore.

4 AFTER YOU READ **Work in pairs to answer these questions.**

1. Why do people like to go diving at Yonaguni?

2. Who discovered the rock formations at Yonaguni? How?

3. What did Masaaki Kimura originally think about the rock formations?

4. What does he believe now?

5. According to Robert Schoch, what caused the rock formations?

6. What is the writer's conclusion about Yonaguni?

5 **Work in pairs.** Why did the author write this text? Tick the best reason. Then explain your choice.

☐ to express his/her opinion about the rock formations at Yonaguni

☐ to persuade tourists to go diving at Yonaguni

☐ to explain different theories about the rock formations at Yonaguni

☐ to describe the history of Yonaguni

6 **Discuss in groups.**

1. Look closely at the photo. Which theory do you agree with? Why?

2. Do you know of any other underwater discoveries? Are they natural or human-made? What do you know about them?

3. Oceanographer Robert Ballard said, 'There's probably more history now preserved underwater than in all the museums of the world combined.' Do you agree? Why? What can we learn from artefacts found underwater?

VIDEO ▶

① BEFORE YOU WATCH Discuss in pairs. Look at the names of famous creatures. Discuss what you know about each one. Can you think of any others? Why do you think people find them so interesting?

> Bigfoot   El Chupacabra   Dracula   Yeti

② Work in pairs. You are going to watch a video called *Loch Ness Monster: Mystery Solved?* What do you already know about the Loch Ness Monster? Compare it with the creatures mentioned in Activity 1.

③ WHILE YOU WATCH List three words that describe the images of Nessie. Watch scene 4.1.

④ AFTER YOU WATCH Work in pairs to answer the questions.

1. When was the first sighting of the Loch Ness Monster?

2. Who was Marmaduke Wetherell?

3. When did a photographer take a picture of the Loch Ness Monster underwater?

4. What did Wetherell's stepson confess?

5. What are the two theories about a recent satellite photo?

6. Why do some tourists still visit Loch Ness?

5 **Work in pairs.** Why do you think that Wetherell created a fake photo? Why would he want people to believe that he saw the Loch Ness Monster?

6 **Work in groups.** What might make you believe a legend like Nessie's? How can you find out if a story is real or not? Discuss different ways that you can check facts and find evidence that something is true.

Urquhart Castle on Loch Ness, Scotland

7 **YOU DECIDE** **Choose an activity.**

1. **Work independently.** Imagine you visited Loch Ness and spotted Nessie. Write a paragraph about your experience. Describe what you saw, how you felt and what you did.

2. **Work in pairs.** Create your own legendary monster. Think about where it lives, what it does, what it looks like and who has seen it. Then write a short newspaper article about a sighting of this monster.

3. **Work in groups.** Prepare a short presentation about the Loch Ness Monster. Use some of the information from this video and some from your own research. Include your own ideas about the truth behind the legend.

GRAMMAR 🎧051

Past simple: Describing past actions

When **did** the village **sink**? It **sank thousands of years ago**.

Last October, divers **discovered** a shipwreck in the Indian Ocean.

In 1912, RMS *Titanic* **set off** from Southampton, UK. The ship **didn't arrive** at its destination.

Nautilus **reached** the Gulf of Mexico **the day before yesterday**.

GREAT UNDERWATER DISCOVERIES

1857	1934	1943	1960	1985	2012
James Alden discovers the Monterey Canyon, an underwater valley in California.	William Beebe makes the first underwater exploration of the ocean in a bathysphere.	Jacques Cousteau and Émile Gagnan invent the Aqua-Lung. It lets divers breathe underwater.	The *Trieste* travels to the Mariana Trench, the deepest part of the world's oceans.	Robert Ballard finds the wreck of the RMS *Titanic*.	Film director and explorer James Cameron becomes the first person to travel alone to the bottom of the Mariana Trench.

1 **Read.** Use the information in the timeline to write five sentences about important underwater discoveries.

More than 30 years ago, Robert Ballard found the wreck of the Titanic.

_____

_____

_____

_____

2 **Work in groups.** Use the photos to tell a story. Say when the action in each photo happened.

> A ship set off on a journey 150 years ago.

> Because of a terrible storm, the ship never arrived at its destination.

WRITING

When we provide information on a topic, we may talk about more than one idea relating to that topic. When those ideas are different, we can use the following words to show contrast:

although	but	even though	however	instead

1 **Read the model.** Work in pairs to identify how the writer contrasts different points of view. Underline the words.

In 1922, a man named Martin Sheffield said he saw a strange creature in Nahuel Huapi Lake in Patagonia, Argentina. It had a long neck and the body of a crocodile. Since then, many other people have said that they've seen the same creature. The local people call it *Nahuelito*. But what's really there?

Some people believe that it could be a plesiosaur – a marine dinosaur. Around 30,000 years ago, the lake was part of the Pacific Ocean. It's possible that as the climate got warmer and the lake formed, the creature stayed there. However, dinosaur experts think this is impossible because dinosaurs were extinct thousands of years before the lake formed. Other people think that the creature is actually a secret submarine. Although this is an interesting idea, it doesn't explain how the submarine got into the lake and why it has been there for nearly one hundred years. A third theory is that Nahuelito formed because of pollution in the water. But the Nahuel Huapi Lake is not very polluted, so this theory seems unlikely.

Some people don't believe there is anything strange in the lake. Instead, they argue that people are looking at pieces of wood or even sheep swimming in the water. Even though it isn't the most exciting theory, it may be the most sensible!

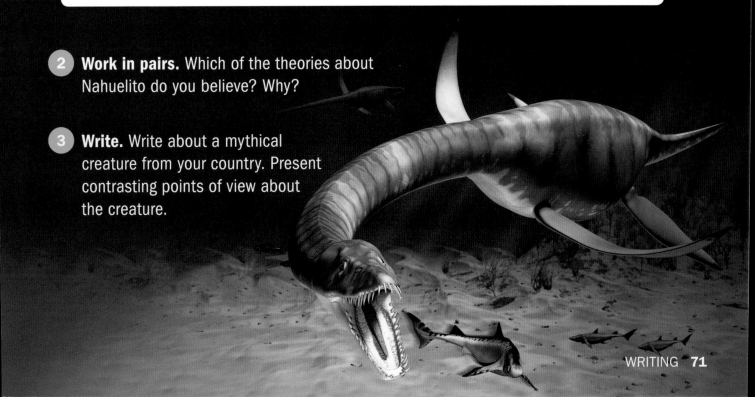

2 **Work in pairs.** Which of the theories about Nahuelito do you believe? Why?

3 **Write.** Write about a mythical creature from your country. Present contrasting points of view about the creature.

Be Curious

'If you don't have questions about where you're going, then you're not going to be able to answer them or learn new things.'

Katy Croff Bell

National Geographic Explorer, Oceanographer

1. **Watch scene 4.2.**

2. Think about the places you go and the things you use regularly. List three places or things. How much do you know about them? How could you find out more?

3. Choose a place in your region, and make a list of questions that you have about it. Ask about its history, architecture, uses and the people who go there. Then talk to people in your community to get answers to your questions.

Make an Impact

1 **Plan and write a blog entry about underwater exploration.**

· Use the Internet to research popular sites for underwater exploration. Find information about a place you would explore and how you would explore it.

· Imagine you explored this place. Write a blog entry saying how you prepared and what your expedition was like.

· Publish your blog entry. Respond to questions or comments on it.

2 **Plan and give a presentation about an underwater city.**

· Find out about an underwater city. Collect photos and drawings.

· Organise your information into a poster or computer-based presentation.

· Give your presentation. Respond to your classmates' questions.

3 **Investigate a local body of water.**

· Choose a body of water near your home.

· Find out about the animals and plants that live in this environment.

· Make a model or a poster to show what you learnt about the body of water and what lives there.

The *Nautilus* Expedition to the Cayman Islands

Hi! I'm Talita and this is my blog! Enjoy!

Day 1: 15th August

Wow! I can't believe I'm actually here on *Nautilus*! I'm one of five very lucky students taking part in *Nautilus's* four-day expedition to the Cayman Islands. We had a talk from the expedition leader, Dr Katy Croff Bell, about where we're going and what we'll be doing. Oh, and all the safety stuff as well, of course! I look supercool in my life jacket ... NOT!

Day 2: 16th August

What an amazing day! In the morning, we met Dr Robert Ballard, who discovered the wreck of the *Titanic*! After lunch (mahi-mahi!), we had a tour around *Nautilus*. We looked at the labs, and we went up to the bridge – that's where the captain of the ship works. I even got a chance to steer the ship! (Don't worry, Mum, we're still heading in the right direction ... I hope!) Later, we learnt about Hercules – a remotely operated vehicle, or ROV. This robot has so much electronic equipment that I'm amazed it's all waterproof!

Day 3: 17th August

This morning we appeared on the *Nautilus* Live website and talked to school students around the world about our expedition. It was amazing – I feel like a real celebrity now! (Except for the clothes ... and the money ... OK, maybe not an actual celebrity, but it was really cool.) The afternoon was NOT cool, however. There was a big storm, and we all felt very seasick!

My team

Day 4: 18th August

This morning was beautiful and the sea was calm. Perfect for a dive! Unfortunately, it was Hercules, not us, who got to go diving. What a lucky robot! In the afternoon, we arrived at Grand Cayman. Although I'm sad to leave the *Nautilus* team (especially Hercules), I'm excited to explore the islands and the waters!

ROV Hercules exploring underwater

2 **Discuss in pairs.**

1. In your opinion, what was the most exciting activity the students did on *Nautilus*?

2. Would you like to take part in an activity like this? Why or why not?

3. Do you read blogs regularly? If so, what kinds of blogs do you like to read? What can you learn from them?

3 **Connect ideas.** In Unit 3, you learnt about the impact of technology on our lives. In Unit 4, you learnt about underwater exploration. How are those topics connected? How can technology help us to learn more about what's underwater?

4 **YOU DECIDE** **Choose an activity.**

1. Choose a topic:
   • connecting with people virtually
   • exploring virtually

2. Choose a way to express yourself:
   • a blog entry
   • a short video diary
   • a poster

3. Present your work.

Unit 1

The schwa (/ə/) sound

1 **Listen.** Notice the pronunciation of the vowels in the underlined syllables. 🔊 **110**

vege-ta**-ble**   **pur-**ple   re-pre-**sent**

Vowels in unstressed syllables often have the schwa sound. Schwa is a relaxed /uh/ sound. The symbol in dictionaries looks like an upside-down *e* (/ə/).

Many common suffixes, or word endings, are unstressed.

ner-vous   **na-**tion

Unstressed suffixes often have the schwa sound. The schwa is the most common sound in the English language.

2 **Listen and repeat.** Circle the unstressed syllables with a schwa sound. 🔊 **111**

pop-u-**la**-tion	**dan**-ge-rous	con-**nec**-tions
ex-**am**-ple	sit-u-**a**-tions	**hos**-pi-tals
de-**li**-cious	at-**ten**-tion	tra-**di**-tion-al

3 **Work in pairs.** Complete the sentences with words from Activity 2. Then listen and check. Take turns saying the sentences correctly. 🔊 **112**

1. People have ___connections___ with colours. For _____ , green makes people feel calm.

2. A _____ colour for weddings is white.

3. About five per cent of the _____ is colour-blind.

4. Walls in _____ are not usually painted black or other dark colours.

5. People pay _____ when they see the colour yellow. It's used on traffic signs to warn people of _____ _____ .

Unit 2

Pronunciation of -s endings

1 **Listen.** Notice the different pronunciations for each -s ending. 🔊 **113**

The -s ending has three possible pronunciations. It sounds like:

- *iz* when the final sound of a verb has a s, z, x, sh, ch or j sound. These sounds add another syllable to the word.
- *s* when the final sound is *f, k, p* or *t*.
- *z* when the final sound is a vowel or any other consonant.

iz	*s*	*z*
washes	sleeps	says
raises	looks	gives
dances	helps	reads

2 **Listen and repeat.** Listen again and write the word you hear in the space. 🔊 **114**

1. Jill ___sleeps___ regularly. She _____ to bed early.

2. Lack of sleep _____ your mind. Your body _____ cells to combat illness as you sleep.

3. Jack usually _____ up late. He rarely _____ enough sleep because he _____ TV late at night.

3 **Work in pairs.** Write each verb from Activity 2 in the correct column. Listen to the completed table to check your answers. 🔊 **115**

iz as in *teaches*	*s* as in *talks*	*z* as in *says*
	sleeps	

Unit 3

Have to

1 **Listen.** Notice the pronunciation of *has to/have to* + verb. 🎧 116

She <u>has to do</u> some research online.
They <u>have to be</u> careful.

The word *has* ends with a *z* sound and *have* with a *v*, but when they are followed by *to* to suggest obligation, the final sounds usually change. They sound like *hasta* or *hafta*.

Got to is sometimes spoken informally after the short forms *'ve* (have) or *'s* (has). It sounds like *gotta*.

You<u>'ve got to</u> (*gotta*) try this new site. She<u>'s got to</u> (*gotta*) get a new computer.

2 **Listen and repeat.** Then complete the sentences. 🎧 117

1. You _____ *have to* _____ be careful online.
2. He _____ get a new phone.
3. I _____ go offline now.
4. She _____ be more polite.
5. We _____ remember so many passwords. There _____ be an easier way to access our accounts.

3 **Work in pairs.** Take turns discussing the situations. Use *have to* or *got to*.

> You have to tell your friend to be respectful.

1. Your friend is mean online. (*has to*)
2. An unfamiliar person keeps contacting you. (*got to*)
3. Your mother wants to be your friend on a social-media site. (*got to*)
4. You're constantly using your smartphone. (*have to*)

Unit 4

Verb *use* vs. *used to* + verb

1 **Listen.** Notice how *use* is pronounced when it's a main verb and when it's in the modal phrase *used to*. 🎧 118

They didn't <u>use to</u> have many tools.
Researchers today <u>use</u> high-tech tools.
I <u>used to</u> see whales in the winter.
I <u>used</u> binoculars to get a closer look.

When *use* is a main verb, the *s* sounds like *z*. When it's in the modal phrase *used to*, it's pronounced like a *s*.

2 **Listen and repeat.** Circle the pronunciation of the letter *s* in *use/used to*. 🎧 119

1. He used to live near the sea.	(s)	z
2. His family used their neighbour's boat.	s	z
3. We didn't use to swim much.	s	z
4. I used to collect small sea creatures.	s	z
5. I would use a jar to collect sand.	s	z
6. I used two of your tanks for the dive.	s	z

3 **Work in pairs.** Make sentences with *used to* and any of the phrases that were true about you in the past, but aren't true now.

> I used to swim in the sea every day. I didn't use to play football.

swim in the sea	play (a sport)
watch (TV programme)	play (an instrument)
eat (food)	love (subject)
walk to school	(your choice)

Irregular Verbs

Infinitive	Past simple	Past participle	Infinitive	Past simple	Past participle
be	were	been	leave	left	left
beat	beat	beaten	lend	lent	lent
become	became	become	let	let	let
begin	began	begun	lie (down)	lay	lain
bend	bent	bent	light	lit	lit
bet	bet	bet	lose	lost	lost
bite	bit	bitten	make	made	made
bleed	bled	bled	mean	meant	meant
blow	blew	blown	meet	met	met
break	broke	broken	overcome	overcame	overcome
bring	brought	brought	pay	paid	paid
build	built	built	put	put	put
burn	burnt	burnt	quit	quit	quit
buy	bought	bought	read	read	read
carry	carried	carried	ride	rode	ridden
catch	caught	caught	ring	rang	rung
choose	chose	chosen	rise	rose	risen
come	came	come	run	ran	run
cost	cost	cost	say	said	said
cut	cut	cut	see	saw	seen
deal	dealt	dealt	sell	sold	sold
dig	dug	dug	send	sent	sent
dive	dived	dived	set	set	set
do	did	done	sew	sewed	sewn
draw	drew	drawn	shake	shook	shaken
drink	drank	drunk	shine	shone	shone
drive	drove	driven	show	showed	shown
dry	dried	dried	shrink	shrank	shrunk
eat	ate	eaten	shut	shut	shut
fall	fell	fallen	sing	sang	sung
feed	fed	fed	sink	sank	sunk
feel	felt	felt	sit	sat	sat
fight	fought	fought	sleep	slept	slept
find	found	found	slide	slid	slid
flee	fled	fled	speak	spoke	spoken
fly	flew	flown	spend	spent	spent
forbid	forbade	forbidden	spin	spun	spun
forget	forgot	forgotten	stand	stood	stood
forgive	forgave	forgiven	steal	stole	stolen
freeze	froze	frozen	stick	stuck	stuck
fry	fried	fried	sting	stung	stung
get	got	got	stink	stank	stunk
give	gave	given	strike	struck	struck
go	went	gone	swear	swore	sworn
grind	ground	ground	sweep	swept	swept
grow	grew	grown	swim	swam	swum
hang	hung	hung	swing	swung	swung
have	had	had	take	took	taken
hear	heard	heard	teach	taught	taught
hide	hid	hidden	tear	tore	torn
hit	hit	hit	tell	told	told
hold	held	held	think	thought	thought
hurt	hurt	hurt	throw	threw	thrown
keep	kept	kept	understand	understood	understood
kneel	knelt	knelt	wake	woke	woken
knit	knitted	knitted	wear	wore	worn
know	knew	known	weave	wove	woven
lay	laid	laid	win	won	won
lead	led	led	write	wrote	written

Giving a presentation

1 **Listen and read.** 🎧 131

Adam: Good morning, everyone. Today, we'd like to talk to you about technology.

Amalia: The focus of our presentation is smartphones. We'll begin by listing the different uses of smartphones.

Adam: The next thing we'd like to talk about is how often teens use smartphones. Please look at this graph. Notice that most teens use their smartphones for over four hours a day.

[...]

Adam: In conclusion, smartphones can be both helpful and harmful. Does anyone have any questions or comments?

Beginning	Middle	End
• Good morning/afternoon, everyone. • Today, I'd/we'd like to talk to you about ... • The focus of my/our presentation is ... • I'll/We'll begin by ...	• The next thing I'd /we'd like to talk about is ... • Please look at ... • Notice that ... • Moving on, ... • Any questions?	• In conclusion, ... • And so, ... • Does anyone have any questions or comments?

Asking for and giving information

2 **Listen and read.** 🎧 132

Julia: Hey, Carlos. Could you tell me what the maths homework is?

Carlos: As far as I know, we just need to study for the test.

Julia: I wonder what's on it. Do you have any idea?

Carlos: Well, I heard that it's all of Unit 10 and the first part of Unit 11.

Julia: Thanks!

Carlos: Sure. I'd like to know if we'll be able to use our calculators.

Julia: I don't know.

Asking for information	Responding
• Can/Could you tell me ...? • I'd like to know ... • I wonder ... • Do you know? • Do you have any idea?	• I've heard/read that ... • As far as I know, ... • I'm not sure, but I think ... • I'd say ... • I don't know.

Interrupting

3 **Listen and read.** 🎧 **133**

Mr Silva: Alberto Santos-Dumont wasn't just a flight pioneer. He also helped make wristwatches popular among men! Using a pocket watch was not practical on a plane, so he asked his friend Louis Cartier for help.

Robert: Excuse me, Mr Silva. Can I ask a question? Could you spell the last name?

Mr Silva: Of course. It's C-A-R-T-I-E-R. OK. Back to the story. Cartier then built the first pilot wristwatch! Santos-Dumont wore it ...

Robert: Sorry to interrupt, but how did Santos-Dumont help make wristwatches popular?

Mr Silva: Great question, Robert! Santos-Dumont was a very popular person. People started noticing his watch and asking about it.

Interrupting	Interrupting to ask a question or add information	Interrupting someone who interrupted you
• Excuse me. • Sorry to interrupt. • Sorry, but ...	• Can I ask a question? • May I say/ask something? • I'd like to say something. • Can I add something? • I'd like to comment on that.	• OK. Back to ... • I have something I'd like to add. • Can I continue?

Agreeing and disagreeing

4 **Listen and read.** 🎧 **134**

Lin: I think we should do a video for our project.

Chang: I agree.

Mei: No way! Not again. We did a video last time. Why don't we do an online presentation?

Lin: I'm not so sure. Presentations can be boring.

Chang: Actually, I think it's a great idea. Presentations don't have to be boring. We can add music and sound effects! Maybe we can do a bit of both. We can do a short video and include it in the presentation.

Lin: I guess so!

Mei: Exactly! A presentation *and* a video!

Agreeing ⟵   ⟶ Disagreeing

• You're absolutely right. • Absolutely! • Of course! • Exactly!	• I agree. • You're right. • That's true. • I think so, too. • Me, too. / Me, neither. • I think it's a great idea. • That's a great idea!	• I guess so. • I suppose so. • I see what you mean. • That could be. • Maybe. • I see your point, but ...	• Yes/Yeah, but ... • I don't think so. • I'm not (so) sure. • I know, but ... • Not really.	• No way! (informal) • I disagree. • Absolutely not!

Making and receiving phone calls

5 **Listen and read.** 🎧 135

Mr Alonso:	Hello.
John:	Hi, Mr Alonso. It's John. Is Ben there?
Mr Alonso:	Hi, John. Yes, he is. I'll get him for you.
John:	Thanks!
Mr Alonso:	Hello?
John:	Hi, Mr Alonso. It's John. May I speak to Ben, please?
Mr Alonso:	Hi, John. I'm sorry, but he's busy at the moment. Can he call you back?
John:	That would be great. Thank you!
Mr Alonso:	Goodbye, John.

Greetings		Asking to speak to someone	Responding		
• Hello. • Hi, (Mr Alonso).	• It's (John).	• Is (Ben) there? • May I speak to (Ben), please? • Can I talk to (Ben)?	• I'll get (him) for you.		• Thanks.
			• (He) isn't here. • I'm sorry. (He's) not at home. • (He's) busy at the moment.	• Can (he) call you back? • Would you like to leave a message?	• That would be great. • No, thanks. I'll call back later.

Apologising

6 **Listen and read.** 🎧 136

Natalie:	Did you send Aunt Anna a birthday card?
John:	Oops. I forgot it was her birthday.
Natalie:	I didn't either. I'm terrible with dates.
John:	I can't believe I forgot it. I'm usually good at remembering birthdays.
Natalie:	Oh! My mistake. Her birthday is next Friday.
John:	That's a relief!
Natalie:	Sorry!

Apologising	
• Sorry. • I'm sorry. • Excuse me. • Oops.	• My fault / mistake. • I can't believe I did / said that. • I'm terrible with dates / names.

Responding to news

7 **Listen and read.** 🎧 137

Good news

Fatima: I have some good news to tell you.

Adil: Really? What is it?

Fatima: Those paintings that we entered in the upcoming art show were accepted!

Adil: That's great news!

Fatima: I know. The show is next week. Well done!

Adil: Wow! That's fantastic!

Fatima: I know. I can't wait.

Adil: Congratulations! I can't wait to see your work.

Fatima: Thank you! I can't wait for the show.

Good news	
• Congratulations!	• That's great news!
• That's fantastic!	• Well done!
• I'm so happy for you.	• Lucky you!

8 **Listen and read.** 🎧 138

Bad news

Fatima: Uh-oh.

Adil: What is it?

Fatima: I have some bad news to tell you. I'm sorry to tell you this, but your painting didn't make it into the art show.

Adil: Oh, no! What happened?

Fatima: Your entry arrived late.

Adil: Oh, no, that's awful.

Fatima: I know. I'm so sorry.

Adil: Oh well. That's a shame. Next time, I'll make sure I send it in plenty of time.

Fatima: If there's anything I can do, let me know.

Bad news	
• Oh, no!	• That must have been awful / terrible.
• How terrible / sad / awful!	• That's horrible/ a shame / awful.
• I'm so sorry to tell you / hear that.	• What a shame / pity!

Begin by saying:

Polar bears have white fur.

Correct by saying:

Cats can see colour. They just don't see as many different shades as humans do.

Begin by saying:

Flamingos are pink.

Correct by saying:

The Golden Gate Bridge isn't red. It's a special shade of orange called 'international orange'.

Begin by saying:

The Golden Gate Bridge is red.

Correct by saying:

There are no colours in black light. Black is the colour you see when there is no light. White is the colour you see when blue, red and yellow light are mixed together.

Begin by saying:

Cats can only see in black and white.

Correct by saying:

Bulls are colour-blind! They get angry when people move suddenly or fast.

Begin by saying:

Bulls get angry when they see the colour red.

Correct by saying:

Flamingos aren't pink. They're grey. They get their pink colour from eating a lot of pink shrimp.

Begin by saying:

Black light is made from a lot of different colours all mixed together.

Correct by saying:

A polar bear's fur isn't white. It's clear. It reflects the light, and this makes it look white.

Start

It's _____ brightest colour in the room.

What colours are _____ books in your bag?

She is _____ only girl in our family.

_____ moon is very bright tonight.

I want to buy _____ new computer.

DANGER!
Lose a turn.

I had _____ apple for breakfast.

GOOD LUCK!
Move forward 2 spaces.

She's _____ most intelligent girl in our class.

BAD LUCK!
Move back 6 spaces.

Are you _____ student at this school?

_____ colour blue is very popular around the world.

Many restaurants use _____ colour red.

Is that _____ plane in the sky?

I love swimming in _____ sea.

BAD LUCK!
Move back 2 spaces.

He lives in _____ small house in Buenos Aires.

My cat is _____ cat sitting on the rug.

Finish

155

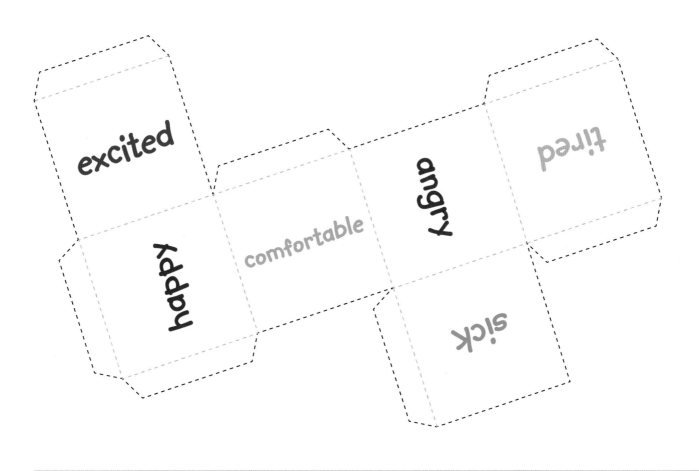

Unit 3 Cutouts Use with Activity 3 on page 47.

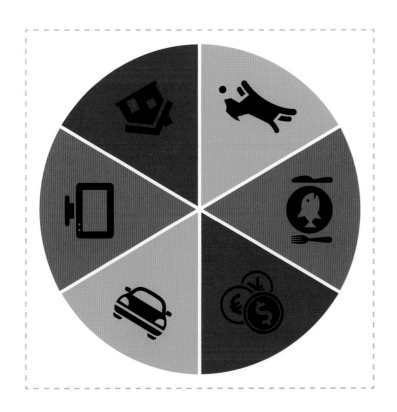

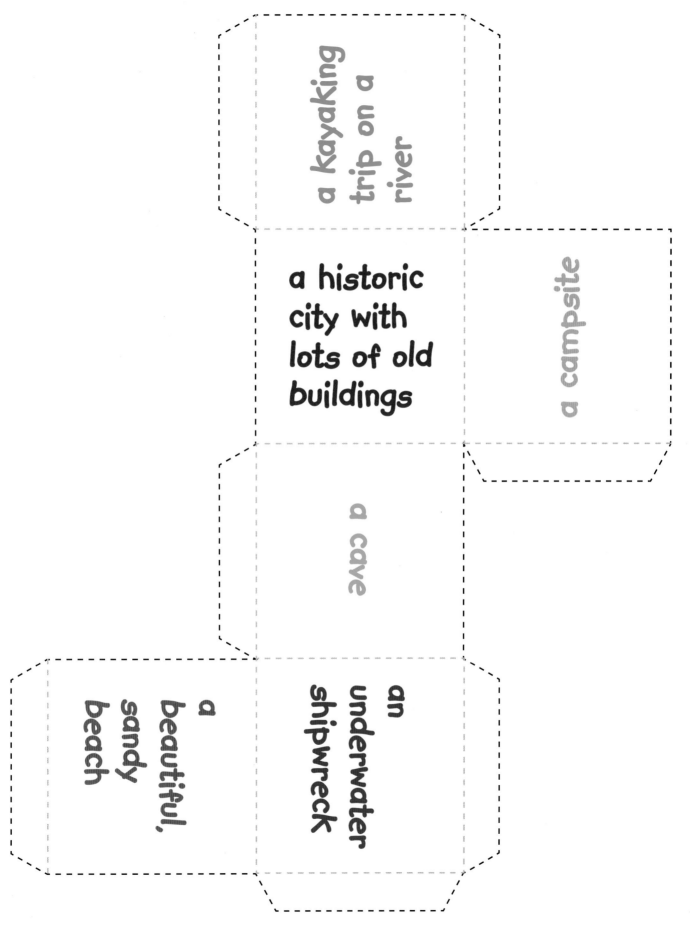

a kayaking trip on a river

a historic city with lots of old buildings

a campsite

a cave

an underwater shipwreck

a beautiful, sandy beach